THE LIMITS OF SOFTWARE

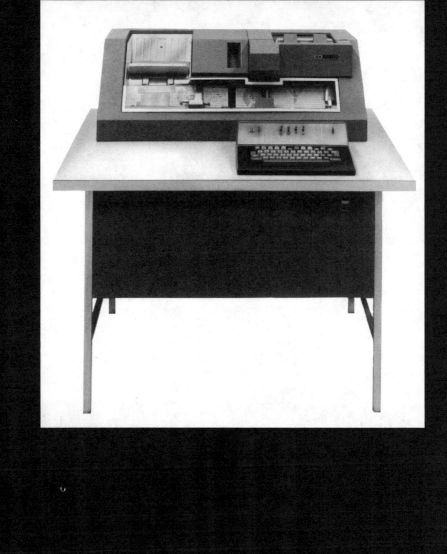

THE LIMITS OF SOFTWARE

• • •

People, Projects, and Perspectives

ROBERT N. BRITCHER

ADDISON–WESLEY
AN IMPRINT OF ADDISON WESLEY LONGMAN, INC.

Reading, Massachusetts • Harlow, England • Menlo Park, California
Berkeley, California • Don Mills, Ontario • Sydney
Bonn • Tokyo • Mexico City

Permission credits appear on page 214, which is a continuation of this copyright page.

The publisher offers discounts on this book when ordered in quantity for special sales. For more information, please contact:

Corporate, Government, and Special Sales
Addison Wesley Longman, Inc.
One Jacob Way
Reading, Massachusetts 01867
(781) 944-3700

Library of Congress Cataloging-in-Publication Data

Britcher, Robert N.
The limits of software : people, projects, and perspectives / Robert N. Britcher.
       p.   cm.
Includes bibliographical references (p.
      ISBN 0-201-43323-0
1. Computer software. I. Title
QA76.754.B75   1999
005.3—dc21   99–24951
                    CIP

ISBN 0-201-43323-0
Text printed on recycled and acid-free paper.
1 2 3 4 5 6 7 8 9 10—MA—0302010099
First printing, June 1999

For J.H.

CONTENTS

• • •

PART II

FOREWORD

• • •

I can't believe how hard it has been for me to write a foreword for this book. Normally, I do my homework on the subject I'm to write about; then I sit down at my word processor, and the words seem to flow from my mind to my fingertips. But not this time.

This is no ordinary book. And it deserves an extraordinary foreword. That's the problem, I believe. It's hard to commit yourself to doing something extraordinary, and then just sit down and have it happen.

Why is this not an ordinary book? Because Bob Britcher is not an ordinary writer. This book is not like anything else you've ever read on the subject of computing. It's part storytelling, part history, part art, part science, part philosophy, part logic—all entwined around the subject of computing and software. To be honest, I don't know whether or not you'll like this book. But I hope you'll be curious enough to give it a try. In the end, you may come to love Britcher's writing, as I do. He may well be the only Renaissance man writing in the computing field.

What's in the book? A collection of anecdotes. A collection of facts and opinions. Some thoughts on the origins of the computing field. Some thoughts on where the computing field is going now. Personal insights on computing's foibles and computing's achievements. Personal insights on one of the largest and most spectacular computing failures in the history of the field.

Britcher worked on the U.S. Federal Aviation Administration's (FAA) Advanced Automation System (AAS), which he calls "the greatest debacle in the history of organized work." He describes in fascinating insider detail the many-faceted failures of that doomed project, coming to the conclusion that the project "brought out the worst in all of us, the thousands who worked on it . . . its atmosphere was slavish and mindless . . . we learned nothing from it."

So this is a book about a particular failed project, right? Well, no. There's far more to it than that. Take Britcher's semi-imaginary playmates, Harry and Clinton, foils through whom Britcher speaks to us readers with sometimes outrageous and sometimes poignant belief sets that, one suspects, are not quite his own or that he is not quite ready to claim. And yet, as time passes and we keep turning the pages of the book, Harry especially becomes a dominant character, and in the final chapter he becomes a tragic figure; we readers find ourselves saddened by a character who we knew was not quite real but who we sense symbolizes what Britcher may feel is the encroaching cloud of darkness over this new age of technology.

Oh, and those wonderful stories of Britcher's—the computer that melted one night, known ever after as the "crispy critter"; the program listing that disappeared into a garbage dumpster and had to be retrieved. Or the wonderful images—Britcher being shown an early windowing system, where in one window "the protagonist [in a movie being shown there] was sucking the blood out of some innocent, while [in another window] I contemplated my next sales call."

In the final analysis, I think I'll remember best the times Britcher shares with us about building software. "Developing software correctly is difficult. Developing vaccines and medicines without side effects is difficult. . . . Neither enterprise will benefit from shortcuts."

It's time to bring this foreword to a close. It wasn't easy to write. I'm not sure it does justice to Britcher's book. What I hope I've accomplished here is to raise your curiosity to an extremely high level, high enough to cause you to proceed eagerly into the rest of the book. I think you'll be glad you did.

ROBERT L. GLASS
Fall 1998

PROLOGUE

· · ·

I live in a housing development, but I work in a town. The town has no churches, no schools, no hospital. But it has neighborhoods, a park, a square, shops, eateries, banks, parking garages, picnic areas, bus stops, great oaks, and conifers. There is a farm nearby.

My office is across from the farm, in a corner of the fourth floor of one of five brick, dormlike buildings. There, every workday, hundreds of us organize our thinking around a large computer project. We work apart but interact as if we need each other. We do. Occasionally, important things happen. Last spring a cardinal flew into my office window, killing itself. A few months later, Janice went to Paris to live, about the time Albert's wife had twins. Someone—I don't remember who—returned a book I thought I'd lost.

One day, hiking between buildings, I ran into a fellow I had seen often but hadn't spoken to for years. Dan. He told me his life had changed. It was ten in the morning. The clouds were full, but the sun was bright and I couldn't see well. The farm looked unreal. I was spooked for a moment. Then I went on to a meeting. I remember a day like that as a child: the sky, the air, the farm, a man on his way to work, feeling it might not last. Later that week I learned Dan had died.

Dan and I had played golf in the IBM golf league. In the 1960s, he worked in IBM's punched card plant in Washington, D.C. Another golfing pal who worked there told me Dan's cancer might have resulted from the dust and chemicals. Now when I think of punched cards I think of Dan.

Dan studied Chinese. He enjoyed looking at derivations. He lent me his copy of *Chinese Characters*, by Dr. L. Wieger, S.J., which I stuck with for about a week. I learned that the symbol for hoe combines the symbol for village and a third of a mile. It is the 166th radical in K'ang-hsi. I also learned that there is no symbol for computer or computer program. My friend Shu explained that the symbol for computer could be derived from the 173rd radical, the symbol for rain, lightning, and electricity, and from the 130th radical, the symbol for brain. Electrical brain. To get programming, or program, she said, add the 194th radical, the symbol for ghosts. It is hewed of the same markings as brain. Since Buddhism it has come to mean an unknown that spreads.

There is something ghostly about computer programs. Like smoke, they pass through programmers and into computers, where they evoke and create more programs that will pass through other programmers and other computers, all the while changing. Like the ancestors of the Chinese, they resonate great authority. The natural world echoes within their loops. I should say our loops, for their behavior is governed by the thinking of programmers, who record them in the same symbols we use to write our wills and love notes.

Programs soften the line between the natural and the artificial. Man's thoughts inhabit the factories and chapels he builds. But these are made from his thoughts, not of them. With computer programs and the functions they enact, man's thinking *is* the arch, the window, the lathe. Without appearing so, every program is a new machine. A steam engine, a lever, a telephone, is invented every few minutes. No factory need be overhauled to change a lamp into soap, a piston into a combine. A programmer can write a program and then change one symbol, and a new machine is born. Adam Smith could not have foreseen such rapid specialization.

Computer programs are now called software. The term *software* has all but eclipsed the earlier terminology. Software has come to mean much more than the stuff of programs. Animation, video games—all sorts of multimedia offerings march along under its banner.

The limits of software were brought painfully home to me with the collapse of the FAA's Advanced Automation System, the largest civilian computer project ever attempted. It promised a complete modernization of our nation's air traffic control system. Development of the computer system, begun in 1981 with a series of studies, ended in 1994. Some of the equipment and software have found a home in other initiatives. But the project as a whole failed, largely because of our thirst for automation and a belief that the easier life is a better one.

Software was once not so glorious. Computer programs performed simple tasks, converting analog signals to digital form, printing reports, filing data, arithmetic. Few promises were made; few people were involved. Some were trained in engineering or science. Most had very little to go on but their instincts for workmanship and this: they wanted to build something that would last. They helped put man in space, control air traffic, and solve difficult mathematical problems.

In recent years, software has virtually taken over. Weapons, communications, banking, recreation, education, politics, and medicine all ride atop the quiet symbols turned out by the million every week. The few programmers are now many. But methods have not advanced. Worse, in many quarters today, sound methods practiced thirty years ago are being ignored. The emphasis has shifted away from dependability. The concept of permanence has seemingly evaporated. Technology has encouraged speed. This applies to the development of software as well. What began innocently enough has turned into the latest form of alchemy.

It seems there will be no end to it. Unlike earlier forms of technology, software is both invisible and easy to proliferate. One can witness the emergence of a nuclear power plant, contemplate its possible consequences, and take a stand against it. That cannot happen with software. Its side effects are upon us before we know it. We cannot see them in the making. Objections are coming along, but it is late in the game. Officially, we are in love with this latest form of automation. Both major U.S. political parties embrace computer technology and software. The information highway will unify black and white, rich and poor. Ordinary citizens have spoken with their money. Today, dairy cows are rigged with sensors so that software can determine their payload. Technology is no longer constrained to the academic and industrial planes. It's on the farm and in the inner city.

What can we do about it? Nothing. What would we do about it? Most of us would do nothing. Our pensions are tied up in the stocks of Microsoft, Netscape, IBM, Sun, and Intel.

This book describes how software is written, who writes it, and the direction software development has taken. It is in two parts. The first describes some of the defining elements of computer programming, in the context of the early systems, developed in the 1960s and early 1970s. The second describes the new era: software as the stuff of high expectations and money. This happy marriage has led to one disappointment after another. The book culminates with the FAA's Advanced Automation System, a bitter failure that set the FAA back a dozen years.

The book is both personal and technical, but largely personal. In software the two are bound more tightly than in any other form of technology. The book is an entertainment aimed at the truth. As such, it combines reportage, history, characters, dialogue, memoir, quotation, stories, and allusion. Sven Birkerts writes in *The Gutenberg Elegies*, "You have a better chance of connecting with the present if you abjure realism . . . make the irreality of the present part of the subject itself. [In today's world] the deeper truth of things can no longer be expressed in sequential realistic narrative." So, read this as you would a story—but a true story.

DRAMATIS PERSONAE

(in order of appearance)

Janice   A colleague on my current project

Albert   A colleague on my current project

Dan   A colleague and golf partner, now deceased

Shu   Raised in Taiwan, one of IBM's most versatile programmers

Gil Slater   The virtual stage manager and guide through the book

Clinton   A colleague who worked large government jobs and now works within the wave of the Web — a 55-year-old among kids

Patricia   Whom I have known virtually all my life, and who is one of the unknown pioneers in programming large systems

Billie   One of many religious programmers I have worked with

Amanda　　A programming technician—a job that is not easy to find these days

Harry　　The protagonist of the story; his life story reflects the shifting nature of programming and software

Ed　　A pure programmer, who still prefers coding in assembly language

John　　A colleague with whom I teach software engineering management at Johns Hopkins University

Roper　　A software development manager who managed programmers for three decades, beginning in the 1960s

Joe　　One of the FAA's best 9020 computer operators

Ved　　A young programmer on the Strategic Air Command's Digital Network project

Mahlon　　Ved's manager, who started with me on the FAA's 9020 System

Gary　　A lifelong friend who practices law in Gettysburg, Pennsylvania

Lee　　An IBM project manager who ate paper

George　　A Korean War veteran, a standout football player at Iowa State, and a longtime IBM project manager

Mike　　A man of many talents, including programming in Ada

Julius　　The lab manager on NASA's Space Shuttle project

T.V.　　Also called H., started programming in the 1950s and later became a philosopher

Larry	A fine man who spent years along the Mekong Delta working for IBM
The Major	A project manager for the U.S. Department of Defense
Charlie	A talented sportsman and artist living in Washington, D.C.
Roy	A friend through grade school, high school, college, and beyond
Tom	A mutual friend of mine, Gary's, Charlie's, and Roy's
Jenny	On the Advanced Automation System project, the IBM software development manager's aide-de-camp
Harmon	One of IBM's lead programmers on the Advanced Automation System project
Sydney	A human factors expert whose behavior embodies that of the Advanced Automation System project
Marie	Harry's wife

The characters listed above are fictional, although they are based on people I have known.

Note: The pronoun *he* and the possessive form *his* are used in places throughout the book. They are used in the general sense of anyone and connote no gender. In other places, the pronouns *he* and *she* and their respective possessive forms are used explicitly, as appropriate.

ACKNOWLEDGMENTS

• • •

I owe a good deal of thanks to Bob Glass for his years-long support of this project; to David Childs and his vision of computing; to Dennie Walker, whose career at IBM spanned the entire history of air traffic control automation; to all the reviewers, both personal and professional; to Michael Leister for his design concepts; to my editor, Deborah Lafferty, who encouraged and helped me throughout; and to the artists, editors, and marketing representatives of Addison-Wesley.

But it is not the practitioners alone who are so moved. A thousand years in the making, the religion of technology has become the common enchantment, not only of the designers of technology but also those caught up in, and undone by, their godly designs. The expectation of ultimate salvation through technology, whatever the immediate human and social costs, has become the unspoken orthodoxy, reinforced by a market-induced enthusiasm for novelty and sanctioned by a millenarian yearning for new beginnings. This popular faith, subliminally indulged and intensified by corporate, government, and media pitchmen, inspires an awed deference to the practitioners and their promises of deliverance while diverting attention from more urgent concerns. Thus, unrestrained technological development is allowed to proceed apace, without serious scrutiny or oversight—without reason. Pleas for some rationality, for reflection about pace and purpose, for sober assessment of costs and benefits—for evidence even of economic value, much less larger social gains—are dismissed as irrational. From within the faith, any and all criticism appears irrelevant, and irreverent.

—DAVID F. NOBLE, *The Religion of Technology*

Transportation and communications advanced, bringing to Aunt May's door the woes of the world.

—William Gaddis, *The Recognitions*

PART I

• • •

<Gil Slater: former editor of *ATM* and (of late) habitual
journal writer.>

Journal Entry 14:

Looking back, it seems to me there have been three mini-epochs
in the brief history of what we now call software, discounting the
early use of computers as a research tool. Starting in the '50s with
the Defense Department's Semi-Automatic Ground Environment
system, and moving through the '60s with the space program, the
air traffic control system, communications, and defense systems,
the term *automation* was taking on a new meaning. With the war
in Vietnam, cities burning, popular music terrifying parents, few
noticed the beginnings of what has become front-page news.

Epoch 1: Hundreds of programmers punched millions of
cards to build the FAA's first national system, a system written three
times, spanning the administrations of Kennedy and Ford. And
hundreds—and hundreds elsewhere—learned a lot about programming large systems.

Epoch 2 ('70s by and large) marked by smaller computers,
software applied to businesses like publishing, banking. Large-scale
projects flourished and many failed, forgetting that the systems
completed in Epoch 1 were often a matter of national commitment
and succeeded often by brute force. Technology outpaced programming and management techniques. The rise of the industrial programmer, video terminals, high-level languages, databases.

Now ahead—Epoch 3, projects of enormous size, reengineering the old and much new. Programming can't keep up with
expectations. The FAA's Advanced Automation System was on the
horizon in 1980 when I married for the second time. Pushing the
limits. Marketing overshadows both theory and practice. Gates and
the Internet.

1
. . .

EARLY SYSTEMS

*Many difficulties had to be surmounted before the
screw was a practicable thing.*
—H. G. WELLS, *The Outline of History*

Atlantic City sits on a ten-mile sandbar called Absecon Beach. It is
the home of the Miss America pageant; the world's first boardwalk,
which opened in 1870; and some of the poorest people in America.
It is also a wet place. In 1962, the resort was almost lost to a hurri-
cane. In 1969, I went there to work at NAFEC, the Federal Aviation
Administration's National Aviation Facility and Experimental Center.

In 1969, NAFEC was a compound of white two-story, weather-
board buildings, raised about a foot above the sand soil to prevent
flooding. Most of the buildings are gone now.

NAFEC had been a naval air station. Situated along Route 9,
it looked like a foreign post. The barracks were tucked under tall
pines. Radars and other navigational gear dotted the great yards. On
the perimeter were runways large enough for a C-5A to practice

touch-and-go landings. There were two new buildings. Building 149 was located just off Amelia Earhart Drive near the runways. Made of cinderblock, Building 149 housed the computer complex. It was constructed for the new wave of automation that began to appear in the mid-1960s: the en route 9020 System and the terminal area Automated Radar Tracking System, or ARTS. As the 9020 System project expanded, a second building, Building 270, was hastily erected. Made of aluminum and tin, it looked out of place among the old wooden barracks.

ARTS is a typical acronym. Although all fields use acronyms, the computer and software fields revel in them. All computer systems and the projects that spawn them are given shorthand names. They start out as a convenience, but they take on more significance. They become pet names for those who work on them, like the names we give to loved ones, or to baseball teams—the Yankees became the Yanks, then the Bronx Bombers. Although our involvement with computers and software seems to dilute our feelings, computer projects, like any project in life, take on a personality. Sometimes we have great affection for them—usually when we look back on them. Sometimes, in the heat of what seem like impossible deadlines, we think of them as battle campaigns.

The man in charge of NAFEC was Commander Buck Commander. He and his wife lived on the base in a graceful white house near the front gate. Every so often his voice could be heard over the loudspeaker warning of some official visit. Otherwise, things at NAFEC were very unofficial. It was a long way from Washington and a short way to the beach. But the men wore shirts and ties and the women wore skirts or dresses. The attire suggested earnestness. Everyone worked hard. The development of the 9020 System and the ARTS was a 7-day-a-week, 24-hour-a-day proposition.

My friends and I worked on the 9020 System. I was told that it was one of IBM's premier projects. The 9020 is a computer, a multiprocessor to be exact. It is several computers running in concert, sharing common storage elements. The 9020 is so large that it would fill a gymnasium. In the 1960s it was fast, but it runs a hundred times slower than one of today's workstations.

A variation of IBM's System/360, the 9020 was specially built for the FAA in the early 1960s. As the name System/360 suggests, computers were evolving from machines to systems. System/360, for example, unified the computer architecture, the operating system, the programming language, and the operator's language.

By 1970, computing *systems* were commonplace. These architectural ensembles made programming large systems easier. In many cases they made programming them possible. System/360 changed the landscape like locomotive-powered railways. Travelers, once isolated in caravans, became passengers. The programmer, once encumbered by the details of his journey, could now tend to the business of algorithms, the computer incidental to his work. As with trains, many programs could ride together and arrive at about the same time; multiprogramming it was called then. With a system beneath them, programmers were no longer just writing programs — they were enriching what was already there. An evolutionary epoch was launched.

I worked on the 9020 System for four and a half years, most of them in Building 21. An officer's club some twenty years earlier, it was repainted just before I arrived. This was a yearly custom. By 1969, the paint was as thick as wallboard. The painters never took the trouble to tape the window frames, so the windows were stuck shut.

The floors buckled from the dampness. On windy days, the building rocked back and forth. Cigarette smoke soiled the air. Weather permitting, we propped open the doors on both floors. Computer listings were piled in the halls, and the offices were thick with them. Punched-card boxes were stacked everywhere. Most were annotated in crayon. Some contained a work in progress. Some were debris. To be sure which, you had to look inside. Asking someone would not do.

The office next to mine had been the shower room. Larger than most rooms, it was as hot as the nearby beaches in summer.

The elevated chain-drawn window could not accommodate an air conditioner. The drain in the center of the floor drew unoccupied chairs to it. During the day you could hear the chairs run.

The north end of the first floor had been hurriedly renovated. It once had been a solarium. Now it was a bullpen of a dozen or so offices, separated from each other by six-foot Plexiglas, which at times became "nets" for paper-wad volleyball. (Work moved along deliberately then. The hours were long, but they could also be slow. One clever programmer, not to be defeated by the occasional boredom, captured flies and deployed them with small tissue signs, like the banners hauled by the small planes that passed along the nearby beaches of Ocean City and Stone Harbor. He helped redefine normalcy at NAFEC. You'd walk down the hall with green-back flies here and there, losing altitude under the weight of their trailers that read "Eat at Zaberers," and think nothing of it.)

My office was on the second floor. It was a good walk down the hall and down the steps to the front-door carrel that partially enclosed two keypunch machines and the courier drop. The keypunch machines were used for corrections only: no more than a dozen cards. Except for a few engineers, who wrote small diagnostic programs at the keypunch, programmers wrote their programs on coding pads. At times, coding pads were hard to come by and were hoarded. Each sheet contained a free-form header for names. But each character of a program had to be written in tiny boxes, like those in a crossword puzzle. The boxes ran to 80 columns to match the punched-card format, and you could get about 24 lines' worth of logic or data on a sheet. Often, zeroes came out looking like the letter "O" and ones could be construed as the letter "L."

Coding sheets were sent by courier to Building 9. There, trained keypunch operators staffed a hive of twenty or so IBM 029s. The operators had to deal with the idiosyncrasies of handwriting, and it was unusual to get punched cards back faithful to your intent.

The rules for courier service were as unforgiving as the coding process. The courier's expectations were exact and sovereign. A small table stood next to the keypunch machines, one end of which was labeled "OUT." There, programmers placed card decks and key-punching forms. Every day, these disappeared at 10 A.M. and 2 P.M. From time to time, card decks, card decks wrapped in coding sheets, and listings appeared at the other end of the table, sometimes in unmarked cartons. Cautious programmers knew the courier by name. Although Maurice Cohen held the lowest civil service rating in the U.S. government, a GS-1, he was very conscientious. But he was an easy target when things went wrong. A quiet man, he would say, "What can they do to me?"

In 1969, programs running on the computer were called jobs. This should have given us an idea of what was coming. No one then could imagine that, in just under 15 years, millions of human jobs would be transformed and displaced by computer jobs.

At NAFEC, running a job required planning, good timing, and some legwork. The production line—from programmer to courier to keypunch operator and back, to courier to job entry clerk to computer operator and back again—was not only ponderous but also unreliable. Card decks wrapped in rubber bands were hauled around in boxes packed in an open-air jitney driven by Maurice. The rain was a problem. The life cycle of a program, from the time it was transcribed on coding sheets until an error-free assembly was returned, was measured in days. So programmers prodded themselves to do careful work. It was monastic. Every line of code was read and reread. Every character was inspected. Who would chance an error, when it could mean days lost? The penalty for hurried work was not limited to wasted labor. Computer runs were itemized. The cost of a job was prorated among users. The amount was printed at the bottom of the listing and reported to the department manager. Extravagance—too many turnarounds—counted against you. In time, even the anxious programmer learned to deliberate. He discovered that going faster meant going slower.

For the air passenger public, the slow going paid off. Although prototyped twice, the 9020 System was deployed three years after the specifications were written—an enormous achievement, considering its scale and complexity (more than two million programming statements). The system supports a network of twenty independent air route traffic control centers that manage our domestic airspace. It pulls together the workings of, among other things, radars, clocks, printers, lights, computers, teletypes, communication lines, jets, radio frequencies, cathode ray tubes, air traffic controllers, transponders, and clouds. The 9020 System has flourished for more than thirty years. It is a monument to carefulness.

More, it is a monument to commitment. The 9020 System, like the Mercury and Apollo Space Systems and their successors, and the network of defense systems with a list of names a mile long, and the public telephone system, which is now the telecommunications system and will be renamed again, is among the great works of mankind. But no one will get on a plane to take the vacation of a lifetime to see it. You can't see it. You can't see any of them. Nevertheless, they are monumental, like the Brooklyn Bridge. The evidence is not so palpable. In fact, we take these systems for granted. But within them circulate a generation's motives and energy and workmanship—which, in programming, where malignant errors are ridiculously easy to make, means an almost ruthless bent for perfection and industry. The 9020 System, as part of the greater air traffic and defense system, operates every minute of every day of every year. It can't shut down and it doesn't. It isn't just there, like the pyramids; it's there and it runs.

The 9020 System wasn't the first attempt to automate en route air traffic control. In the 1950s, the IBM 650 drum was programmed to calculate estimated times of arrival at fixes for flights crossing the Indianapolis air route traffic control center. (Fixes are points in the sky, like towns along our highways.) The 650 was a quinary machine. It operated like an abacus. Like Roman numerals, place can be tracked by your fingers alone. The 650 came with 2,000 words of memory. (Once upon a time, a word meant 2 bytes, or 16 bits, as in the 650. Or a word could consist of 4 bytes, as in the 9020.)

A second version of the 650 featured 4,000 words. To use the 650 efficiently, programmers had to know the speed of the drum and the speed of the instructions. There were other challenges. The 650 could get hot. It had no built-in fan, so its door was left open and a floor fan was placed next to it to keep it from overheating.

The printer that supported the 605, a 403 accounting machine, was more powerful than the 650. The 403 had enough relays and storage to run on its own. At night, air traffic controllers would turn it on and watch it print data left in it that afternoon. One controller said it reminded him of the eerie way chickens flapped around his old neighborhood after the landlord axed off their heads.

The flight data reached the controllers from the printer in strips, produced by a device invented one night on third shift. It was called the "cutter and stuffer." The strips were put into tubes and sent off on a pneumatic trough that circled above the controllers. At the right station, the tube was dropped. It would crack as it hit the controller's bench. This, it was said, would keep him alert on third shift—if it didn't knock him out.

We had systems before we had computers. But computers have made systems more popular. Sometimes systems just happen. A passerby, such as a biologist or a historian, may spot currents of activity, notice a pattern here and there, and then declare it a system. There are also near-systems, things working together at times, in some places, but not others. We like to put our minds to these and round them out; then they are fit to call systems. When we inject computers into systems—which is now most of the time—we consider them digital systems, although parts of them are not digital. In my hometown, the Adams County Public Library bought a computer. So the townsfolk call the library the Adams County Library System. It's no longer just a place.

Sometimes we create systems from scratch, like arithmetic or the phone system. We rarely retire them. Mostly we enhance what's already there. We have had a field day with systems since World War II. There are all sorts of systems now, from ecological systems to banking systems. Sometimes these interact, creating a megasystem, as when some cattle crashed through the front window of a bank across town and caused a computer outage. We now have systems thinking and systems analysis and systems engineering. A friend told me that cardiologists are like engineers, sort of mechanical, not psychologically minded. I said that some forms of engineering might be impersonal, but not systems engineering. Systems engineering brings us together as naturally as possible. He apologized, said he didn't mean to step on my toes. Then again, maybe systems engineering brings us closer to machines and moves us farther from each other.

Systems frequently operate inside other systems. The 9020 System was part of the National Airspace System, which is part of the U.S. Air Defense System—at least the military sees it that way. (I should say "The 9020 System *is*. . . ." The system is still around and so is the computer. Although the 9020 central computer was replaced by an IBM System/370 3083 in 1986, the 9020 is still used in the display subsystem. The 3083, an example of how quickly things change in this field, went out of steady production by 1988. Its installation caused the 9020 System to be renamed. It is now called the Host Computer System, so that neither the computer nor the purpose of the system can be identified from the name. I prefer the original name—the one I grew up with.)

Circulating inside the 9020 System are pieces of other national systems: the weather system, navigational system, communications system, the surveillance system, the time system, a logistics system, a flight reservation system, to name a few. The 9020 System uses these systems to calculate arrival times, like the 650 drum at Indianapolis. It also paints the air traffic control displays, or situation displays, with digital radar returns. These the computer annotates with flight IDs and other important information, such as the airplane's altitude, position, and velocity.

People operate within systems, and vice versa. Systems change us, just as we change them. At first, digital radar made the air traffic controllers nervous. They distrusted the computer in the middle. So the FAA kept the original interface, with the radars feeding the displays directly. The displays could present either the digital radar through the 9020, or, as a backup, the broadband, the unfiltered, predigital radar report of a plane's range and azimuth. If the 9020 went down, the displays were flattened to the horizontal. Hand-drawn "shrimp boats" were brought in to replace the digital track and moved around by hand to keep up with the broadband.

Within a couple of years, a backup computer was set down along the broadband path. This was grounds for calling it a system, a backup system called DARC, for Direct Access Radar Channel. En route controllers could no longer revert to broadband. The displays were soon fixed in the upright position. "No more shrimp boats!" Although manual procedures still prevailed in flight planning— the controllers could remove and handle the paper flight strips— surveillance would be fully automated. One computer system would back up another. Not long after DARC came online, and the controllers got used to a fully digital backup, they asked that some of the 9020 functions be added to DARC as well. Despite early resistance to new computer systems, their acceptance is soon followed by demands for more automation.

One of the most difficult aspects of computer systems is changing them. They are always being changed. During the transition, there are at least two versions of the system running, side by side. Systems not only swim inside and around each other; they show up as families, father and son, mother and daughter. Sometimes they come in schools: the previous system, the one before that, the system in the field, the system in the laboratory, the system in design, the next generation. For planners and builders, it is a little like feeding time in the nest. The situation is especially puzzling for programmers, who must keep track of five versions of the same loop.

Systems, like bridges, can rarely be overhauled in place. Maintaining two versions, the current one and the new one, sometimes creates unusual problems. Here is an example of what can happen.

There is a great oak near the New York TRACON on Long Island. The New York TRACON, or terminal radar approach control, is one of the busiest in the world. Each year, about 55 million passengers depart from and land at the airports within its range. The ARTS runs inside the TRACON. (It would be more accurate to say that the ARTS runs through it. The computers sit within the TRACON building, but the system, with all of its aspects, is inside, outside, and all around.)

In 1985, IBM bid on an FAA proposal to replace the New York TRACON computer, a UNIVAC 8300. Our efforts fell short, in part because of the great oak. IBM's strategy was clever: to install a 3083, the computer about to replace the 9020 central computer in the en route centers, and convert the ARTS programs from UNIVAC assembly language to JOVIAL, the language used in the 9020 System. Unfortunately, there was no room in the TRACON for both systems, the current and the new. So IBM hired a firm that specialized in reengineering facilities. After several weeks, they had a design. It required moving some office space and erecting a temporary building on the grounds of the TRACON—after removing the oak tree. This hit a sour note with the FAA. Digging up the oak tree would violate not only the statutes of nature but those of history, particularly the history of aviation. The tree stands near Roosevelt Field, from which Charles Lindbergh made his noble flight across the Atlantic.

A second solution—to create a mezzanine within the TRACON proper—fell upon deaf ears. After the tree proposal, we could not be trusted. What would IBM suggest next? An asphalt driving range? An arcade? A sushi bar? After careful consideration, the FAA disqualified us. The bid went to Sperry-UNIVAC, who stayed with the original computers and upgraded them with semiconductor memory.

Being young and ambitious, I would have sold that tree down the river for a few pieces of gold. But today I'm glad things turned out as they did. Trees seem much more important than computer systems to me now. Despite our penchant for more helpings of automation, more systems in combination until the world is thick with them, I believe trees will outlast them.

Sometimes, when we try to automate systems, to tighten various manual and automatic procedures with programming loops, we can't. In fact, this is the case most of the time.

In 1970, eight North American newspapers formed a consortium called the Newspaper System Development Group. It included the *Washington Post*, the *Toronto Star*, the *Miami Herald*, and several Scripps-Howard papers. The group contracted with IBM to build the Full Page Composition System. From operational concept to its abrupt termination, the project lasted seven years. Along the way, the *Washington Post* fired or retrained its linotype operators, master craftsmen whose parents and grandparents had been linotype operators. In 1975, the *Post's* pressmen attacked the presses. They pummeled them like Chrysler's sheet metal workers hammering a Toyota. It did no good. They would be among the many thousands who would be displaced by computers.

When the Full Page Composition System ended in 1976, Raytheon had produced dozens of composition and makeup terminals, and IBM had written thousands of programs. The specifications had taken years to write and would fill a good-sized bookcase. The project was estimated to cost $15 million. Because it considered the system an investment, IBM did the work for $5 million.

The system, fed by a combination of interactive, batch, and networked inputs, stored the makings of a newspaper in a tremendous database. Every day, raw computer data would be transformed into the next edition. Stories would become articles; text strings, headlines, and captions; and graphics, the picture on page 12. The process was guided by a production controller, a new "systems job."

The Full Page Composition System, dedicated to the task of producing newspapers, was to be paperless. No manual procedures would be permitted. The newspaper staff would not be as fortunate as the astronauts on Apollo 13: when the onboard computer had to be shut down to save power, they copied off the orbit predictions—on paper—so they could fly home.

The system never left the laboratory. There were many problems. Optical character readers were not reliable; graphics scanners, less so. One of the vendors, Singer, was spreading out from sewing machines to video display terminals—with some difficulty. They turned to a company called Omnitext, which later went under. The Page Output Device was never built.

The newspapers could not get together on requirements. The various users competed for attention. The reporters were sure their jobs were decisive in the life of the paper; a Pulitzer Prize can make a newspaper. Management was just as sure—they ran the operation, after all. The marketing force that sold the full-page display advertisements knew better. If it were not for them, there would be no profit. The classified department meant guaranteed revenue. The composing room got the paper out.

To solve these problems, the group divided into subgroups, forming, from the various papers, the news group, the display ad group, the composition and makeup group, and so on. To focus the teams, a blue-ribbon management committee was formed, directed by a gold-star panel, chaired by Dwight Brown from the *Miami Herald*. IBM changed management once; the newspapers, twice.

There were happy moments, however. Newspaper people are intelligent and witty. The representatives of the various papers turned their frustration with computer systems and the acronym-riddled and mysterious software development business into a work of art called *The Lord of Hosts, or The Fellowship of the Quest, with abject apologies to J. R. R. Tolkein.* It ran to over 50 pages and featured adventures like the rite of concatenation, the penetration of the host (a precursor to the 3083), and a rather touching story from the Land of Hardcopie. They turned their fears into humor, a far cry from the fist-pounding antics of military projects.

The project ended like a snapped tape. The newspaper owners had caught on. While IBM and the consortium were struggling to build a grand, integrated system, the separate papers started their own data processing departments and bought in-the-small: a few terminals for the classified department, a package offered by the wire services, a heavy-duty printer, a little something here, a little something there, one step at a time, each taken with the familiar pencil or typewriter close by.

The 1970s were a turning point in the history of dreams. Soon, integrated circuitry would reduce the computer to a speck of sand; new protocols were being developed that would allow programs to run in many machines simultaneously; and graphics would render the action underneath in brilliant colors. The information age was not so much dawning as flaming.

It is tradition in this untraditional software field for everyone to do things his own way. We are still in the prehistoric age. So it is not surprising that, even as the Full Page Composition System was collapsing, the FAA—a few miles down the highway—was planning a system of even greater stature, whose scope would encompass a hundred newspaper systems. It too would absorb new technology; it would nullify old-time jobs and create new ones; it would change the habits of virtually all the workers; it would be totally automated and paperless. Its name at the time was a matter of debate, but by 1980 the designers had settled on something suitable: the Advanced Automation System.

THEORY BEGETS PRACTICE—
OR IS IT THE OTHER WAY AROUND
LIMITS OF SOFTWARE MAY LIE IN ITS COMPLEX ROOTS

Journal Entry 23:

In the '60s, while programmers plowed ahead on large projects, with no big picture, no history to guide them, a handful of mathematicians aimed to make programming more disciplined, mathematical, scientific, formal—they described the objective of their work in one or another of these terms. They believed that programming was only one step ahead of wiring plug boards.

In America, Harlan Mills developed an approach to what became known as "structured programming," although the Europeans beat him to the punch. Mills's tack was simpler than the Europeans', but programmers in the States clung to machine code (or assembly language)—except FORTRAN was OK.

Across the Atlantic, Dijkstra and Hoare and Wirth and a few others were busy with their own methods, which they also called "structured programming." These were men and women who had a working knowledge of formal logic and who claimed that this was crucial to understanding and writing correct programs. I wonder about that. I helped develop the Launch Processing System, which supported the Moon shot, and I didn't know anything about logic. Anyway, their work led to new languages. The '60s was the decade of compilers: Algol became the touchstone for much of the research on computer programming.

Later, Dijkstra developed a formal approach using a very small procedural language, in which the proof led the program. In Mills's approach, the program led the proof. This let our programmers off the hook. We could easily skip the proof.

Hoare, independently, developed another small programming language in terms of axioms and inference rules, and then moved on to proving data representations, which led to the notion of abstract data types, a concept with a deep history in formal logic and mathematics.

2

. . .

THEORIES OF PROGRAMMING

We must grasp this not only generally in theory, but
also by reference to individuals in the world of sense.
— ARISTOTLE, *On the Motion of Animals*

With each passing day, we are living more and more in the Fifth World, the world of software, the world the media calls cyberspace. The number of users is growing steadily and their use more constant. (Are we called "users" to remind us of the utility of computers and computer programs?) Young and old alike are logging on, signing in, downloading, searching, even debugging. Behind the scenes, software runs everything from banking to space exploration. But the number of people who know how software is written is small. Most of us are not talking, or we are saying "Trust us."

Programming is not a science, and there is no theory of programming. If there were, everyone would approach programming the same way. Identical methods would be taught in all universities, as they are for physics and chemistry.

There are theories *about* programming, and theory has informed programming, largely through programming languages. Stumbling upon the source code of LISP or PASCAL, a scholar, with considerable effort and intuition, might be able to puzzle out the tenets of symbol systems or the theory of types. But it's unlikely that he or she would be successful, not because the task is too formidable but because the scholar would soon surrender to the urge to write programs, like the rest of us, and quit the inquiry.

In classical production, mechanization and the division of labor allow builders to proceed without knowing physics. To some degree, programming languages serve that purpose in software. Programming demands very little formal education or training. Automotive workers are trained for months. Yet children can write programs within a few weeks or days after learning the lexical rules laid out before them. They need know little, if any, mathematics.

The question has been asked for some time now: Should programmers apprehend programming as mathematics or, at least, as the application of mathematics? Is it OK to turn out algorithms to automate world banking without having been certified in Boolean algebra? Read the smattering of theory at the end of this chapter and you will know why, when it comes to programming, theory and practice may never be on speaking terms.

THE NEW ALCHEMISTS

In some ways, programming is like chemistry—but chemistry as it was practiced in the era of alchemy. Programs are not unlike molecules. The specification of a protein has much in common with the specification of a large computer program. Both are introduced into the natural world only after they are considered to be structurally fit on paper. Both are tackled in increments that must be checked before continuing. Both are built of a handful of operators that in combination attain unimagined complexity. Even the interfaces between programs resonate like valences; they can be strong or weak, like molecular bonds. In programming, we use simpler names— nothing as mysterious as dichlorodifluoromethane. We usually name programs for what they do, like "Sort," not for their structure and fabric. If we did, the names of programs would be as long as those given to chemical compounds.

Chemistry has a history, packed with theories and years of practice. The early programmers went to work informed by little or no theory—perhaps the theory of computation, if they attended one of the few schools that offered it. There was no recorded history of programming practice. Most of my colleagues had studied no computer science. They had little interest in learning about programming in a formal way. We were paid well to keep our heads down. What we did seemed far removed from theory. The first great computer systems, the 9020 System, the Apollo Space System, the telephone system, were built by programmers who knew little about computers or the significance of programming, nor cared to. They became official programmers eight weeks after learning a few assembler language instructions and some FORTRAN. (In 1954, less than four years after Alan Turing's last paper on computation, John Backus invented FORTRAN. With FORTRAN, programming would look like formula writing, on the surface not too different from high school algebra. A few years later Backus created a language of staggering simplicity. Backus-Normal Form is a landmark in the history of formal languages.) At one time, chemists were launched after just a few weeks of training, knowing only some of the elements that turned up centuries later in the periodic table.

Like alchemy, computer programming has become an admixture of greed and metaphysics. Programmers share some of the alchemists' objectives. There is more than money at work; turning symbols into gold moves us closer to the ultimate. "What better way to emulate God's knowledge," writes the computer consultant Michael Heim, "than to generate a virtual world."

Programming shares some of the alchemists' methods. Long before the periodic table was introduced, alchemists, very scientifically it turns out, combined what we would now call compounds by following the latest process. Great minds were at work on it. Thanks to the economist John Maynard Keynes, who purchased several forgotten journals in 1936, we know that Isaac Newton devoted a good part of his life to alchemy. Newton may have considered himself more of an alchemist than a mathematician or physicist. He subscribed to a number of alchemical tracts. In 1669, he got serious. He bought his own furnace and installed it near his flat at Oxford. After that, he showed much fervor in pursuing his belief that alchemy mirrored God's labors during the creation. Were he alive today, it would be a good bet that Newton would be a programmer. It's unlikely that he'd be an alchemist. In 1980, with the use of a particle accelerator at the Lawrence Laboratory at Berkeley, a bismuth sample was transmuted into one-billionth of a cent's worth of gold. The cost was $10,000.

STRUCTURED PROGRAMMING: THE FIRST GREAT THEORY

There is a programmer in the Royal Society. His name is C. A. R. Hoare, and he lives in Ireland. Hoare is one of the fathers of what is called structured programming. Another was an American mathematician, Harlan Mills.

Harlan Mills loved sports, mostly for their statistics. He was a large, modest man who had a decisive impact on programming at IBM. He was admired by a handful, but most of the rank and file distrusted him because he believed programs are mathematical objects. Mills was also a salesman. He did not invent structured programming—he did not name it, nor define it—as much as sell it.

What is structured programming? Mills and his colleagues asserted that it is thinking about and writing programs algebraically, independent of the computer. Thinking, rather than machinery, is emphasized. Programming constructs, such as loops, can be refined, simplified, and substituted for—as in algebra. In this way, large programs can be written from small ones. "Small blocks of closed spaces to constrain our imagination; a simple topology of values. Not the vast province the machine invites," said Mills. "In a sense, it's a matter of aim." Bobby Jones, the great amateur golfer, put it this way: Build a correct golf swing based on the principles of geometry. Forget about the ball; it merely gets in the way. Likewise, the computer just gets in the way of a programmer's perfect geometry. Mills was a friend of management. He urged programmers to move forward deliberately, in small steps. He was not interested in code; he was interested in correct code.

Structured programming submerges structure and emphasizes behavior. Like a Harold Pinter play, things turn on what is missing. If you like arithmetic, as did Harlan Mills, here is an example. Specify the number "9" and let it mean something, like the number of players on a baseball team. So far, the number "9" has meaning but no structure. Then, with the use of what Mills called the axiom of replacement, the "9" can be expanded or refined. Operators, and therefore structure, can be added. So we have "3+4+1+1." The number of outfielders and infielders, and the pitcher and catcher, what baseball fans call the battery. In much the same way, a programmer might specify "A:=max(X,Y)" — to assign the larger of two values, represented by X and Y, to the variable A. Later, having assured himself of the correctness of this expression, he can refine it: for example, "if X>Y then A:=X else A:=Y." The programmer is easing toward the computer. More structure is added without changing behavior. The crucial step is the last: to verify that the expanded version is equivalent to its simpler specification.

By the early 1970s, programming languages were enhanced, and some new ones were created, to favor the thinking of humans over the structure of the computer. Loops would look more like loops to the programmer and less like a computer instruction. My friend Shu told me that if one were to mandate a culture, or eliminate one, there is no course more certain than to strike at the mind through the eye of language. Last year, a friend told her of the cultural revolution in China. Mao pressed for the return to ancient kanji. The stick figures, predating the writing brush and its flourish, arrest diversity. In time, their use, Mao felt, would attain mandarin standing. Thus, by conformance through language, the individual could not ascend. Programmers got used to writing structured code because the languages insisted on it.

Structured programming got Clinton to Japan. Clinton is a journeyman programmer I have known for years. He once worked for Harlan Mills and taught structured programming. He traveled the world with other apostles.

Clinton went to Tokyo in 1971. There, for two weeks, he taught 20 programmers. He needed a translator. Once in a while Clinton and the translator would have a long discussion when something like "loop invariant" came up. Eventually, the translator would smile and nod his head, and of course he didn't know, but it was time to move on.

Exams were given. Mills wanted to be sure students were qualified to use structured programming. He believed that lives would depend on it. So Clinton gave an exam. Everyone did poorly, except for one student, a young woman. She was the only woman in the class. Clinton thought it was odd to see any women in the class, based on his briefing. He had been told the Japanese reserved professional jobs for men.

After the exams had been handed back and the final lecture had been given, the class invited Clinton to lunch. The next day Clinton took the subway to the office of his newly minted structured programmers. There he was met by the senior member of the staff, who showed him the bullpen where they worked. Their desks stretched back in rows from his desk, like the oarsmen in Ben Hur. Everyone acknowledged Clinton graciously and they all went downstairs to the cafeteria. After half an hour, Clinton asked where the best student was; he hadn't seen her upstairs. The translator seemed a little bewildered at first and then raised his head back with a smile and hummed one of those Japanese high notes. She was only the office lady, he said.

TRANSFORMATIONAL SEMANTICS

Not long after the first computer was built, programming theorists began looking for a way to code programs as pure mathematical relations, using the syntax of formal logic and calculus. If this could be done, programs would be specified as theorems and then proven, like the Pythagorean theorem. More to the point, programmers could be trained as mathematicians. This would lead to professional certification, and programming would achieve high standing in the field of engineering. Programming would take on the character of, say, geometry.

The mathematical theory has not yet panned out. The problem is that mathematics is not concerned, outright, with producing work through machines. That engineers have used pure mathematics for centuries to build machines, roads, and bridges is not the issue. For them, mathematics is an intellectual tool; it is not the material of the machine. The mathematics does not transform; it merely informs.

In the early 1970s, Edsger Dijkstra, a mathematician from the Netherlands, developed what he calls "transformational semantics." It combines the tenets of classical mathematics with the semantics required to program a computer, to command its circuitry to move data in and out, and, thus, to turn a sensor on a spacecraft. These semantics come down to the declaration of variables, the loop, the if-then clause, the assignment of values to variables, and the semi-colon—semantics that flow, as work, but that can also be treated as the elements of a proof.

Dijkstra and C. A. R. Hoare taught transformational semantics at a series of conferences held around the world. A friend, Patricia, attended their First North American Conference on Program Construction in 1986, at Salve Regina College in Newport, Rhode Island. (An earlier conference was held in 1985 at the University of Woollongong in Australia.)

Salve Regina is a college of arts and sciences, run by the Sisters of Mercy. Founded in 1934, it occupies 65 acres on a bluff overlooking the Atlantic Ocean, near Commodore Vanderbilt's mansion. The bluff is manicured green—the grounds of wealth. But the dorms are stark, just the place to do mathematics. For ten days, about a hundred programmers from various companies and universities learned about this promising theory.

Teaching new theories can arouse suspicion and confusion, even acrimony. On the fifth night of the conference, everyone received a manuscript that was slid under the door after-hours. It contained a copy of letters exchanged between one of the students, Walter Tuvell, and Edsger Dijkstra. The last letter, from Tuvell, ran to over twenty pages and was called "Outline of Predicate Calculus with Identity." The students had already seen Tuvell in action in the seminar. Now they could chew on his points at their leisure.

Programming is mostly about logic. So it's natural to worry about the foundations of logic, especially since programs control nuclear power plants at about ten million instructions per second. I read Tuvell's manuscript. He writes with authority: "The foundations of logic are settled. The definitive treatment for users of logic has been written: Bourbaki. The lives of computer scientists would be much easier if they would accept this." Tuvell goes on to mention that Dijkstra has confused object language with metalanguage, among other mistakes.

Dijkstra's rejoinder begins gracefully enough: "Thank you for your letter, which, indeed, created the impression that you don't count 0 among the even numbers." But later he clarifies his position, which can be summarized with his statement that "I do not subscribe to the approach to logic as advanced by N. Bourbaki. In fact, the predominance of Bourbaki in French teaching is one of the most likely explanations of the poor state of French computing science." He went on from there.

Of course, this is all hard to explain. But programming is hard to explain. It would be better if I told you about the landscape near the escarpment and the cocktail party at the mansion on the ninth day where the musicians played Mendelssohn, or about the arrangement of symbols on a page and their evocation of the jetties on the shoreline.

TYPES

C. A. R. Hoare doesn't write much, but what he has written has changed programming.

Hoare prefers to see programs as axioms. In this way, they can be proven correct before running them on the computer. Fundamental to his axiomatic method, and to the pursuit of correctness, is the theory of types. They are called programming types or data types. They, like the other theoretic aspects of programming, are complicated. But it is important to our story that you know just how complicated all of this is. If they are not already, your children will soon be writing programs.

A programming type is a group of things—not everyday things like lamps and books, or the earthworm that crept onto my stoop this morning, but invisible things. Call them forms. If you could see them, they would look like geometric forms: triangles, squares, cubes, trapezoids. You can't see them, and they are covered in no geometry book. But they are forms nonetheless. They endow programs with small parcels of structure and size.

An example of a simple type is integer arithmetic. Today, virtually every compiler embeds this type in its lexicon, so programmers don't have to invent it. The integer type consists of objects—for example, the set of whole numbers; what mathematicians call a bound, the range of possible values, say from 1 to 10; and a set of operations that close them, such as + and −. Typical compilers support addition, subtraction, multiplication, division, and exponentiation, and the allowable bounds are enormous, spanning positive and negative numbers into the millions.

Types scale up. Because a type is an independent structure, it gives programming a clean way to create a module, a concept fundamental to all engineering.

Types go back to the work of Bertrand Russell and Alfred Whitehead, who tried to formalize all of mathematics. Russell invented logical types to sort out one of the paradoxes of infinity, to deal with the mind-bending contradiction of a set belonging to itself, a problem closely resembling the dilemma of Groucho Marx, who claimed that he would never be a member of a club that would have him as a member. We have types because the class of elephants has no trunk and thus cannot be an elephant, so that one high thing can be defined in terms of a lower thing. The anthropologist Gregory Bateson uses this example: "Acceleration is of a higher type than velocity." One name can look down upon another, which can be about another, and so on: a mountain of abstractions.

This hierarchical arrangement is natural for programming. Programmers, like all humans, think in hierarchies. With the concept of types, programs can be built of other programs simply by reference. Thousands of programs can absorb one another by name. We are well on our way to creating the Tower of Babel. It is no longer just a biblical story; it has arrived. The latest programming languages, notably C++ and Java, make quick absorption even quicker. Pick up any magazine or newspaper and you can read about them. Chances are, they figure in your investment portfolio. You can thank Russell and Whitehead.

PROGRAMMING FROM START TO FINISH
IS ABOUT HUMAN BEINGS
HUMAN ELEMENT SUSPECTED IN AIRPLANE CRASH

Journal Entry 26:

I'm writing this journal during my off-hours. Those are the hours in which I am confined to my chair, usually in the mornings, to give my back a chance to acclimate to the day. I have chosen this approach over narcotics. After my first week I realized that I could spend the better part of four hours watching videos, or television, or reading, or writing, or listening to my wife's mother. I chose reading and writing. Physically, these activities are more uncomfortable for me. Psychologically, they are the least uncomfortable.

Journal Entry 27:

If the roots of programming are complex, what are we? I saw a headline the other day: Human Element Suspected in Airplane Crash! Suspected? Humans came up with the idea of manned flight, built the airplanes and radars, invented the computers that run the software that controls airplane traffic on the ground and now in the cockpit, pilot the planes—and on. Even if lightning hit the plane, the human element caused the plane to be there in the first place. We don't give ourselves enough credit.

I read about the debates of cognitive scientists: What is consciousness? I know. *Consciousness* is a word created by humans, in this case English-speaking humans, to describe something humans know nothing about. Now, scientists think they are onto the secrets of life. Can they explain this: in the 1930s, on a car track in Pennsylvania, Jimmy Concannon threw a wheel, and in a crowd of 11,000, killed his mother.

The real scoop on programming and software is the human element. I didn't know Alan Turing or John von Neumann or the other inventors, but I've known plenty of programmers. We are just like everyone, part this, part that. Except we have to deal with enormous complexity, which springs upon us only after we are too far into what started out to be kind of fun—coding an algorithm and watching it run on a machine. Then it's too late and it all becomes work, very stressful work.

3

. . .

THE HUMAN ELEMENT

*I hardly think that any of us would be willing even
to enter a motor-car, if the driver informed us that
he drove without allowing himself to be distracted
by traffic regulations, but in accordance with the
impulses of an exalted imagination.*

—Sigmund Freud,
New Introductory Lectures on Psychoanalysis

Billie had Jesus beside him when he wrote programs. He mentioned
this once or twice in my office. On his lunch break Billie would walk
to the white pines on the south side of our building, sit for about half
an hour, and read his Bible. Sometimes he would stop by in the
afternoon and chat. His hobby was carpentry. He said that when he
retired he wanted to devote full time to it.

Several of my programming friends are carpenters. They tell
me it compensates for their long days manipulating texts. Working
with wood, you can see where you've been and where you are going.
And then there's the feel of the wood, its shape and smoothness. Its
destiny is in your hands.

On a NASA project, I wrote a program that interfaced with a program of Billie's. For some reason—I no longer remember why—he was given my program to maintain for a while. I was proud of my program. I had worked on it for months. I was especially proud of the commentary. Each section of code was neat, code interleaved with narrative, both drawn clearly down the page. There were no jump lines, no widow lines. I was careful to separate the comments from the source statements so they could be changed independently. In my absence, Billie deleted all the comments. He said he did it to shorten the listing—Billie felt comments were an encumbrance. More to the point, for that short period of time, it was *his* program, and he could do what he wanted with it.

I was more than a little angry at Billie at the time. But he was doing what is natural: it is a simple matter to change a program. Billie deleted all of my comments in seconds because it pleased him to do it. This sort of thing is not obvious to theoreticians, and it probably does not happen in universities. But it happens a lot in industry, particularly on large computer systems, where programs are not owned by one programmer for very long. This is often why programmers work very hard to get the code right, their way. They know their time with it is short and someone else will do what he wants when he gets it.

Computer programs are not like fine furniture. When a carpenter sees his neighbor's grandfather's clock, he may or may not admire it. But it's unlikely he would grab his tools and start changing it. From time to time it has been suggested that programs be put under warranty and that programmers sign their names to their work. This might be effective as long as the rules of ownership were strict, precise, and public.

In the end, I restored our program—Billie's and mine—to its original state. I stayed on the project a couple of more years. Billie went on to teach programming to IBM secretaries, clerks, and security guards who wanted to change careers.

I knew Amanda before I knew Billie. We worked together on the 9020 System and played tennis. Amanda was not religious in any orthodox way, but she spoke in tongues. Frequently, she had back problems, which she arrested by banging her head against the nearest wall. She and her husband, George, owned a farm in Egg Harbour with a rooster, whose name was also George. George the husband, according to Amanda, had not worked a day in his life.

What stands out about Amanda was her job: she was the first near-programmer I knew. For years she administered the specifications of the JOVIAL COMPOOL, the tables and arrays that underlay the logic of the 9020 System. If the logic were like people, the COMPOOL is like the land. Over the course of the project, new variables and records would spring up here and there, like houses and streets in suburban Washington. Amanda watched over them, like the planning commission. Amanda's job was crucial. In those days, any program could access any data. There was little or no regard for security or what programmers called storage protection.

But for all her responsibility, Amanda was not allowed to touch "code"; that is, she could change arrays, but loops were kept from her. There were rules. Programming instructions, with rare exception, could be written only by college graduates. The variables they changed were left to technicians.

Most of the programmers and near-programmers I worked with were not as eccentric as Amanda or Billie, but many were obsessive. I surely was. Through hard work I overcame it, but it took years. In the early days I carried my source code around with me and read it. I read code while watching television, eating dinner, and, occasionally, in the car, a habit I promptly abandoned after I drifted onto a field off Route 9 one evening.

I didn't like debugging. I have no great affinity for machines. This put me in the soft camp. I was a soldier but not a marine. Marines spent hours and hours in the computer room and the lab, debugging everything. I joined them from time to time. But I couldn't keep up. So I was not welcome. It's like the stories that soldiers tell about combat. The guys at the front resent the guys in the rear, who resent the guys at headquarters, who resent the guys back home, who resent the guys who aren't in the army.

At NAFEC, if you worked a hundred hours and third shift and found other people's bugs, you were really something. The best programmer there died after a few years of this: a heart attack. He wasn't a real marine, even though he worked their hours. He was just a good man doing his job. He couldn't say no. Shortly before he died they gave him an award.

I met Harry at NAFEC. He lived in one of the IBM neighborhoods, two doors down from me. Most of us bought or rented homes near other IBMers. We had not taken up residence in south Jersey as much as we were bivouacked there. Harry never won awards, but he was a master programmer. Before he was a programmer, Harry was a mathematician. He was born with a silver spoon in his mouth, but things never went right for him. His mother was a reformed Catholic. Before that she was depressed for many years. His father spent a lot of time at work, but he ruled the house, even from the office.

Harry told me that, in college, he lived in a small apartment off campus and kept all his books in the bathtub. He said he changed after college; he began to think differently. Then he had some kind of a breakdown, or, as he put it, a recognition. He washed every day and organized his life. He bought suits and put his books in bookcases. He dated. Maybe it was the space, he said. When he got more space, he changed. Harry worried about space and time a lot. That's why he was drawn to programming.

Harry was very careful and neat. He dressed like T. S. Eliot, neat as a pin. He wore three-piece suits, even on the graveyard shift. Harry's programs were like poems. He claimed there was value even in the way they were laid out on the page. As in poetry, the image and thought and feeling came through in the spaces.

(Poets and programmers no longer dress like T. S. Eliot. Does dress affect the way we program? The historian Fernand Braudel writes that fashion is not a trifling thing: "The Persians are not anxious for new discoveries and inventions; they believe they possess all that is required in the way of necessities and conventions for living and are content to remain so. Tradition is a strength and a straitjacket. Perhaps if the door is to be opened to innovation, the source of all progress, there must first be some restlessness which may express itself in such trifles as dress, the shape of shoes and hairstyles?" Who knows what part waistcoats played at Oxford, for example, where for centuries the world was run and nearly ended by men whose only qualification was that they could read Homer in the original?

Then there is John Cheever. Before he made his mark as a novelist and short story writer, he lived in a modest West Side apartment. There, every weekday morning, he would put on his only suit and have breakfast with his wife. Then he would join the other commuters and ride the elevator to the basement, where he had rented a small room. The room contained a desk, a chair, a typewriter, a waste can, and several ashtrays. Once safely in the basement room, Cheever would remove his clothes, down to his underwear, and write. After work, he would put on his suit and join the returning commuters. Today's programmers working at home do not go to all that trouble. (One fellow I know told me that he codes naked.)

Harry was quiet. He looked quiet, like he had something on his mind, something abstract. Passing him in the hall, I would think about the plaque that marks Freud's home in Vienna: "Reason is quiet. —Seneca." After programming, Harry went to Morocco with his wife, a Frenchwoman. Harry wrote to me off and on over the years. In Morocco, they sold telephones and sculpted. Later they settled in France, in Lorraine, in the town of Metz. When Harry lived in America he made cellos. He loved wood.

I kept some of Harry's programs. I have them in a box under my desk at work. They tell a story. There is a beginning—a preparation—then an unfolding. Reading his programs, I was unaware of machines. Machines are not quiet. They rattle and sometimes break. Harry's programs do not rattle, and, as far as I know, they did not break. Harry taught me to read through a program, then study it. It is something to be felt first, then learned, he said. All of the great programmers know this. Harry wrote very few programs and he made very few cellos, not because he quit early but because he took the time to get them right.

PROGRAMMING IS LIMITED BY OUR ABILITY TO DESIGN PROGRAMS AND DISCUSS THE DESIGN CLEARLY

Journal Entry 33:

I feel better this morning. I am thinking about my father and mother. My father was a design engineer. I never clearly understood what that was. My mother was an English teacher. My father told me once that if you cannot write down a design for something, chances are you can't build it. At least build it right. My mother told me the same thing. She said, If you can't write a single theme sentence describing your paragraph, you're not ready to write it.

The term *architecture* is tossed around now in software. I'm not sure how it applies. I took a course in architecture in college. Most schools don't offer such a course, unless they specialize in architecture. I remember my professor telling us about cities and buildings, and, oddly enough, the Gettysburg Address. He talked about the automobile and human desires, for expression, for freedom, for invention. He told me he was once stuck in traffic on a rainy afternoon on Fifth Avenue in New York, with hundreds of cars fuming at the gills, "mixing carbon monoxide and desire." That was in 1975. He wondered if Henry Ford could have envisioned such a scene, such toxic frustration.

When I think about the Year 2000 problem, I think about two things. The first is that architecture, in part, is about the future, about building something that will last and not curse our descendants. The second is the abbreviation we use for the Year 2000 problem: Y2K. When I was programming in the 1960s, we had a project manager, an engineer in the old sense. He did not understand the binary system. When statistics were presented to him about how much computer storage was being consumed, we had to translate the number 1,048, or 1K, which was then common shorthand for 2 raised to the tenth power, into 1,000, which is 10 raised to the power of 3.

We used to argue with him furiously. He didn't get it. Of course, all of our capacity numbers were off. But in those days when 32K was a lot of storage, it didn't seem to matter much. When I look back, he may have been onto something. Today, when the papers and magazines and programmers and software managers refer to 2K, they obviously mean 2,000. Marketing has won out over mathematics.

Where were we then and where are we now? Then, programming suffered from managers who had been engineers but didn't comprehend programming. Now we suffer from managers who have been programmers but know nothing about engineering.

4
. . .

DESIGNING

The practice of architecture is directed by a few general rules.

—EDWARD GIBBON,
Decline and Fall of the Roman Empire

Before programs are written, they should be considered, or thought about. They should be designed. Virtually all computer programs *are* designed. Whether or not the design is written down is another matter. Perhaps the title of this chapter should be Conveying Designs.

Complex things cannot be built successfully without a plan, without some form of note taking. Many of the first programmers did not believe that computer programming was that complex, given their singular ability to puzzle over algorithms and master them. That belief continues today. Intellectual prowess is an important myth among programmers. At Microsoft, acknowledging Bill Gates's phenomenal programming ability is an important part of the corporate culture. Of course, in the long run, the myth is just that. Successful programmers are those who can hold in their minds but one or two loops and are pressed to write down a design, to see the larger picture, the context, as designers of kitchens and schools and golf courses must do, before they build.

Programmers starting out in industry face two problems that, by and large, no one has defined for them, much less prepared them to conquer—problems far beyond the difficult task of writing a correct procedure, an accurate and fault-tolerant algorithm, a dependable and usable program. In a system of programs, how does one program fit with other programs and the values they may change? In other words, what is a module? More to the point, what is a *good* module, one that will remain intact beyond the life of its creator? Then, what does it mean to design a module? The second problem, almost insurmountable on large systems, is how the ensemble of modules fits into the real world. To respond to the second problem is to ask this question: What does the word *architecture* mean in the digital world?

I want to tackle the two problems in reverse order. My approach to the second problem is philosophical. If it were procedural, I would want to change it every two or three years. I can only ask this question: What is architecture? I cannot define it with any precision.

(For a fuller and more literate treatment of this question, I recommend reading *What Is Architecture*, by the British architect Paul Shepheard. Shepheard not so much answers the question as begs it. He writes in the preface, "My purpose here is not to arrive at a definition for the sake of consensus." He quotes a few of his students and colleagues: "Architecture is a metaphor! says one." "Architecture is a computer program! says another." "Can nuclear physics help? Can literature?")

My approach to the second problem—what is a module and how is it designed?—is also not simplistic. The example I use leans toward mathematics. I make no apology for that. I did not invent programming; it *is* mathematical, and therefore difficult and enigmatic.

WHAT IS ARCHITECTURE?

"Consider the ripples in a patch of wind-blown sand. This pattern is a recognizable and constant pattern, because it is a truth about the laws which govern sand and wind."

What would Christopher Alexander, the teacher and architect of cities, say about the laws that govern computer programs and their relationship to humans, this new meeting of the artificial and the natural? He writes that "architecting derives from a pattern language; the concept of a balanced pattern is deeply rooted in the concept of feeling. The fact is that Chartres no less than the simple farmhouse, was built by a group of men, acting within a common pattern language, deeply steeped in it of course. It was not made by design at the drawing board."

We seem to have no such pattern language for architecting computer systems, not because we lack experience, although that may be part of it, but because we have no feeling for them. Cathedrals and cities are dwellings. Humans dwell within them and upon them. They enrich us and we enrich them. This cannot be said of computer systems. They appeal to the nonfeeling in us, the habitual and the obsessive. Lacking a genetically felt pattern language, we do not know how to present and preserve computer system architectures, nor convey the sense and sensibilities of architecting to our successors. This may be one reason we rarely write them down. Another is that conveying the architecture of computer systems is not easy in the first place. A universal language and form for documenting the architecture of computer systems may someday emerge. The Department of Defense sponsors such work. Committed professionals are busy defining protocols and standards, which, if not undermined by the vicissitudes of the private sector, might prevail.

Architecture is not merely the parts of a system in relation to one another, or a collection of modules, but the relationship of the whole ensemble to its environment, to us, to the land, to politics and economics, and to the future. Architecture rearranges the future.

Once, an air traffic controller wrote the identity of an aircraft on a shrimp boat that he moved with a stylus across a flattened display. Now, the computer annotates and moves the annotation with each sweep of the radar, without which air travel could not have swollen beyond what we could have imagined decades ago, which has given rise to the yen for more computer programs.

With the famous Year 2000 problem spreading fear throughout government agencies and businesses, the future is now. Many programs use only two bytes to hold the characters "00," not four bytes, which could specify "1900" or "2000." So, as we approach the new century, will it be 1900 or 2000? In 1966, on the 9020 System, the algorithm that converts month, day, and year to the day of the week was copied from *Scientific American*. But it had a bug. The algorithm did not consider that end-of-century years are not leap years, except for those evenly divisible by 400—as decreed by the pope in 1582. The bug was fixed in 1983.

Architecture is much like the garden by the side of my house that was once a barn. At times, the subject seems like it belongs to anthropology more than to engineering: discovering the mores of a corner, the importance of the wall next to the patch of basil, a lane heading somewhere off into the future, the operations of a beehive, a baseball stuck in a rotted spout; or discovering that a camera's behavior and its structure are changed by the light on a summer porch after a cloudburst. The width of rail tracks can be derived from the width of a Roman chariot.

But architecture can be as mundane as choosing the right programming language. In 1965, IBM chose to write the 9020 System application programs in JOVIAL. JOVIAL worked for most applications; but it was too slow when it came to buffering and storing radar data. An IBM vice president lost his job and the radar programs were rewritten in assembly language, at the level of machine instructions. It is more than thirty years later. JOVIAL programmers have all but died out. Another dilemma: the programs work, but they are written in a language out of joint with the times. Should we change the programs or the programmers?

In the best of worlds, an architecture emerges. Architects dig into the whys and wherefores and weigh the "what must be" against "what cannot be" until landscapes, or machinescapes, become evident, as with jigsaw puzzles. Then forms simply become obvious, the by-product of intent. A baseball is a near-perfect marriage of purpose and form. Its form suggests its use. A toddler finding a ball in his way will try and throw it. A cat will swat it.

Sometimes form results from the unintended, or from side effects. I knew a golfer who developed a hitch in his backswing to ease the pain in his back. It added pace to his whole game, he said. He kept the hitch after the pain disappeared. So many errors were reported within one distributed system that a computer was added to capture and log them. Later the computer became a workstation and a new job was created with a title and a salary code.

Sometimes an architecture is determined arbitrarily, like the snap of a finger. Someone simply declares this or that, because it worked before, because it will sell a computer, or because the popular trend demands it. Sometimes an architecture happens a little at a time, as in decorating a Christmas tree. Its purpose deeply felt, we nevertheless approach the act like children. We throw some tinsel and ornaments on branches, then retreat to take it all in, have a drink, watch the fourth quarter of a football game, then again move in. We do this over and over until time runs out. Of course, great tombs are not built this way.

Sometimes architectures are well planned and then undone. What began with thoughtful analysis ends like a Christmas tree. In the early 1980s, IBM built the Data System Modernization system for the U.S. Air Force to integrate a variety of computer systems and procedures developed to control satellites. Architects worked night and day to fit the programs to the operating system, to processing deadlines, to the computer's storage constraints and its input-output channels and devices, to the failure modes, to the testing and training requirements. But after all of the programs were coded, the computer turned out to be too small. The architecture was renovated a program at a time over the course of a year at the field site, until little was left of its symmetry and balance—just programs wedged into the machine.

No architect can ignore size. Several years ago I read that a compound had been designed that would destroy the AIDS virus. But to produce enough serum to inoculate one person would fill a syringe the size of the lab in which it was synthesized. Many systems are designed that cannot be built. In programming, size is the coefficient of structure: the number of operations times the range of their potential values; the invisible times the invisible. What does a large mathematical space look like? Is it as impressive as the space shuttle or the nuclear power plant near Somers Point, New Jersey? Can we build systems of tens of millions of programming statements? Whether a system is large or small, we, the consumers, the builders, the sponsors, rarely hold anyone accountable for the tenuously built—not like the architects of Babylon, who, standing under their creations for days on end, had to attest to their structural integrity with their lives. There are some who would build a bridge over the Atlantic Ocean, thousands of programs wide and long. It would collapse in the making, invisibly, mysteriously. (After he became psychotic, the great dancer Nijinsky proposed that a bridge be built over the Atlantic, but not made of software.) Such systems are being proposed weekly. The FAA's Advanced Automation System was one such system.

Architecture involves just about everything and everyone: the designers and the builders and the users and those who teach architecture, and programmers unborn, who will change programs that are now just ideas, or who will invent a computer that may change the nature of programming. The designer is linked to the builder of one program, which is linked to the user of another. The safety of aircraft depends on the correctness of the compiler that generates the code, and the correctness of the compiler depends on how and where it was built. The way we are organized to create forms affects the way the forms are organized. The way we are managed affects the way the forms are organized, the way the forms are organized affects the way we are organized, and the way we are organized affects how we manage. These relationships are central to architecture, the way the layout of a town affects the mental life of the children who grew up there.

Architects create rules that strike or strengthen a balance between the photograph on the mantel and the grave behind the house, between the capacity of a computer and the capacity of the people who will use it. In the best-designed systems, the rules are more like the rules for rules. The thoughtful architect specifies only major forms, enough to define the first tenets of a system's behavior, where each function fits with respect to its neighbors and their neighbors. This he does as precisely as possible, so that those who come afterward can, with little difficulty, elaborate the design and, even later, change it. The clearer the architecture, the easier it is to comprehend and the longer it will be preserved.

From 10,000 feet above, the layout of Cambridge, England, looks harmonious, as if conceived by a single mind that honored its major themes: religion and learning. But at street level, the neighborhoods look as if they just evolved. And they did. Custom ruled. The city's architect respected the future builders and inhabitants. They should have their say, these souls, most of whom he will never know.

On the Host Computer System, I laid out the design for a new support system. The original punch card and magnetic tape configuration was to be replaced with an interactive database. I went too far. I specified too much detail. I insisted that one relational database connect *every* element of the software development environment. The subsystem designers and coders soon learned that this elegant solution could not work. Uniformity and commonality have their limits. A simple query took minutes to complete, when a split second was required. Happily, the team proceeded without me. They developed separate databases that could be queried independently. The team succeeded and I learned when to stop.

The rules are not given to an architect, like a bright day on the Mediterranean. It seems to be a matter of discovery, like finding the middle ground between the philosopher's truth and the everyday truth. Constraints and tolerances inhabit variables the way eccentricities inhabit families and towns and clubs. A few needs are unnecessary. Certain behavior is intolerable. Some forms cry out for total independence. Often, too many people are involved. The thoughtful architect respects our desire for machines, yet holds us back. He insists that the artificial be introduced into the natural world gracefully. (The natural, nature, appears to us as irregular; its beauty lies partially in its diversity. Yet its creatures—ants, bees, humans—part of nature's fabric, and quite irregular in form and behavior, build artifacts whose form is largely regular. Nature's builders build objects that are symmetrical, rectilinear, spherical, as if to exclaim "This is our work. Look at it; you can tell we were here." I had thought that there is something paradoxical about this, until Harry pointed out to me that the structure of DNA, the double helix, is quite regular; and perhaps if we looked at the natural world from afar, from God's vantage point, it would appear regular. "We are much too close to see the great pattern.")

The thoughtful architect was a builder who has not forgotten how to build. He is grateful for the chance to bring about quiet steps—whether crossing over from one pattern of behavior to the next, or from one generation of form to the next, or from one apprentice to the next. He imagines where the work will end and travels backward, one step at a time, until he spots the beginning; then he goes forward, taking the shortest route in the shortest time with people who enjoy the scenery. He appreciates geometry *and* teamwork. He honors both the rules of Euclid and the rules of bees.

DESIGNING A MODULE

In the history of programming, few modules have been formally designed. First, there is no universal agreement on what constitutes a programming module. Second, there is no universal agreement on what is meant by design.

Why have modules in the first place? The answer is the same as in classical engineering. A module is a part that can be built and cared for independently. Modules allow work on large projects to proceed with some degree of concurrency. One person or one group can work on one module, while another works on a different module. After each module is found to be working, it can be combined with other working modules. This *is* the way great tombs are built.

Centuries of experience and common sense dictate that a module be specialized, that it do one thing or one set of related things, like the liver or the heart, that it not dwarf other modules in size and complexity nor the ability of the person or persons building it, and that it interface with other modules as simply as possible.

In the early years of industrial programming, in the 1950s and 1960s, the idea of a programming module was not mature. Mathematicians had defined a computer program. A computer program enacts an algorithm, or an effective procedure. That is, given well-defined inputs, a program computes well-defined outputs and completes the job within a time limit that withstands the test of computability. (A number of good books explain the foundations of computation. Joseph Weizenbaum's *Computer Power and Human Reason* remains one of my favorites. It is easy and fun to read. Weizenbaum, for good reason, does not go into the personal lives of the mathematicians whose work gave rise to computers. If you believe that what we do is in large part determined by who we are, you would not be surprised to learn that this most enigmatic epoch of automation, which we are inclined to embrace but know little about, sprung from some of the most brilliant and troubled minds in the history of mathematics. Kurt Godel, whose theorems demonstrate the limits of logic, suffered from depression and he eventually starved himself to death. Emil Post, whose symbol systems paved the way for the concept of the algorithm, was frequently hospitalized for manic-depression. And Alan Turing, whose theoretical work led directly to the development of the modern computer, was a convicted pedophile. After helping win World War II by breaking the Germans' secret code, he meticulously poisoned himself.)

As you might expect, the first programming modules were entire programs: one procedure, one algorithm. Considering that most of these early modules were written in assembly language, modules were often gargantuan—sometimes thousands of statements long—although it was not long before programmers learned to break these into pieces called subroutines.

The design, if it was recorded at all, was recorded on a flow chart. Flow charts could be drawn anywhere, but flow charting tablets were available. They were the size of an easel pad. To constrain the drawing, programmers used plastic templates with cutouts to support decision blocks and input-output operations. Flow charts were not without problems. They helped organize the logic of a program, but they gave short shrift to the data it would affect. And changing a flow chart was painful, sometimes so painful that you wanted to give up and just code.

In the late 1960s, after dozens of large systems had been built and many more had been attempted and abandoned, the module was given serious consideration. And with the module came the concept of design—design in the sense that engineers had practiced it for many hundreds of years: writing or drawing a specification for a module or part or subsystem that captures its intent and structure so that it can be built by someone else. Modularity suggests design, and design suggests abstract specifications. Modules permit many to work together separately. Design permits many to work together at different stages of production. Yet both concepts have value even if there were only one worker and one piece of work. Modularity and design give us mastery over breadth *and* depth.

A professor of creative writing told me about a successful novelist who spent years designing each book, using storyboards. She engineered each novel, defining chapters as one would define modules. She wrote a theme for each chapter. She created scenarios to map the development of her characters across chapters. She developed time lines, annotated events with high-level descriptions, refined themes, "designed the whole damn thing." She repeatedly revised the design until it suited her, until she had a baseline. Then she went to work writing. The professor told me that her novels were among the best he'd ever read. He said she understood that you can't worry about choosing the right word if you're preoccupied with the plot. He wouldn't tell me her name.

By the 1970s, writing designs for programs was becoming popular. Most companies ascribed to some sort of data flow diagramming. Diagrams appeal to people who tend to understand situations graphically. Mathematicians, such as Harlan Mills and C. A. R. Hoare, developed a lexical approach: they insisted that formal languages be used to record designs. I preferred the lexical approach because I felt it was more precise. More important, a formal design language has these advantages: as in any algebra, a problem can be modularized—it can be closed, as mathematicians would say; it is amenable to the techniques of a proof; and it can be mapped to a programming language more easily than diagrams. Studies have been done to determine the effectiveness of the two approaches, but results are inconclusive. The field still turns mostly on opinion.

The technique I learned while at IBM, developed by Harlan Mills, defines a programming module mathematically. His idea was to model a module as a state machine, a concept I will explain in a moment. If used properly, the state machine model results in a module that is, first and foremost, represented as a design; that is, it is specified before it is coded. Second, it is constrained in size. Modest scale is achieved by specifying only those procedures that are related to the data values, or states, they use and modify. The relatedness is everything.

The state machine concept is not unlike organizing a house in terms of its rooms, and beneath that, the things *in* the room. Consider the kitchen a subsystem of modules, where the stove is a module. What we do with the stove is limited and specific to the stove. These are the stove procedures. We boil water on the stove, for example. We freeze water in the refrigerator. The refrigerator is a different module with different procedures. In Mills's concept, it is crucial that a procedure dedicated to one module not modify the data values in another. You would not freeze water on the stove.

We use design models every day. One example, of which I am not an expert, is needlepoint. In needlepoint, graph paper is used to lay out a pattern. Square by square, its color, contrast, and knotting are specified. French knot, continental, half-cross. The configuration varies according to how the needlepoint will be used. Pillows are more forgiving than chair covers. In either case, the details of implementation, the needle size, the thread, the size of the canvas holes, are deferred. The design approximates the actual without imposing a procedure for building it. Here is an everyday example where the form of the design—in this case the graph paper—and the design process at once define the unit of work and spell it out conceptually, the way an artist, in one step, delimits and sketches the landscape he will paint.

In its general form, the state machine is very much like the graph paper used to design needlepoint, except that the state machine is purely mathematical. The word *state* means that, at any moment, a value of the machine, or program, can be known.

A state machine is a special kind of mathematical function, or rule, that computes values. Like the graph paper, it maps values on the x-coordinate (inputs) to those on the y-coordinate (outputs) in some pattern. The pattern is the function. If you wanted to, you could describe a needlepoint pattern mathematically. But who would want to?

Unlike the needlepoint, a state machine remembers. Imagine graph paper with depth, so that each stroke of the pencil could be saved down below. One of the defining aspects of a state machine is that its history can influence the output derived from a given input and rule.

Now think of a game of checkers, which is also laid out in an x-y grid. At any moment in the game, the configuration of the board and its pieces represent the history of the game to that point. The state of the board determines the move of the player in turn. He jumps his opponent's checker. This move (an input) results in a piece being removed from the board (an output), and a new state. The mathematician Alan Turing, whose papers were decisive in defining the theory of computation, showed that all computers behave this way, no matter how they are built. The same could be said of all computer programs.

An intellectual tool like the state machine makes possible the near-impossible: specifying an entire subsystem of an air traffic control system on a page. The designer can decompose the specification one step at a time without losing intellectual control. In successive steps, he algebraically replaces the tracking state machine with those state machines that compose tracking: the mapping of the airplane's planetary coordinates to the air traffic controller's display coordinates; the smoothing of the trajectory; and so on. As each step is derived from its ancestor, the designer demonstrates their equivalence to himself and to others. Thus, the programmer, in deliberate, verifiable steps, moves from the conceptual toward the actual—the program running on the computer—without losing his way.

Today there are a number of design models that projects can use. Programmers can choose which abstract and yet precise model best fits the problem at hand. The object-oriented approach to design—close in spirit to the state machine and the abstract data type—has recently caught on. Aficionados have even created a partial catalog of design patterns within the general model. Inspired by Christopher Alexander (one wonders if he would appreciate his popularity in the field of software?), the authors of *Design Patterns* (Gamma, Helm, Johnson, and Vlissides) identify a method for developing, and give examples of, such patterns. But no approach to design will succeed without designers who are patient and committed to design as an end in itself.

CODE: THE DNA OF SOFTWARE

ALL THAT "SET-UP"— SPECIFICATIONS AND COMPILERS
AND TEST TOOLS AND NAMES AND INTERFACES
AND VARIABLES AND VALUES AND LOOPS AND
IF-THEN-ELSE'S — JUST TO CHANGE AN 8 TO A 6

Journal Entry 34:

Next Day: Gil Slater here! Ex–software manager. It's hard to believe I did that once. When I started, programming was a lot like wiring a plug board. Put a number in a register, shift the bits, store the thing somewhere in storage. Then came FORTRAN. As luck would have it, I went directly from FORTRAN into management. I had to manage programmers who knew more than I did—programming changed so fast. That's been the case ever since.

I never did appreciate the subtleties of programming. I thought coding was the one thing I understood. I found out I didn't even understand that. My son is a programmer. He claims that programming is a form of biology. All those programmers transferring their genetic and neurological codes to the computer. He says the computer code is a reflection of our code.

As a manager, I had to figure out how much work programmers were supposed to do and how fast they were to do it by guessing how much code they could write in a month. My first job I got within 200 percent. We overran something awful. But nobody noticed. The hardware vendors were six months late. Then I got promoted. I told my programming managers that they had to estimate the software size and effort within 15 percent or they wouldn't get a good rating.

They weren't too much smarter than I was; there was no history, no database of programming productivity. So we all fumbled along together. Eventually, we got the ball in the end zone and moved on. The last thing anyone wanted to do was go back and figure out why our reckoning was so far off—no one was paying us to do that. We pretty much kept what we learned to ourselves. I have to say it helped me get ahead. I always liked Gore Vidal's quote: "It's not enough to do well; others must do poorly." So I became a deputy project manager. I worked in the field another 15 years. Near the end, I took night courses in financial management and real estate.

I consulted for a while on the FAA's Advanced Automation System. I didn't understand much of it; it was too complicated. But I was comfortable; mostly because there were more consultants than coders. They didn't know much more than I did. I'm going to write more on that project in my journal, but later.

5

. . .

CODE: THE STUFF OF PROGRAMS

Our methods will be based on the idea of Emil Post
that the "expressions" of a logical system, whatever
else they may seem to be, are in the last analysis
nothing but strings of symbols.
— MARVIN MINSKY, *Computation*

Code is all that matters, according to Ed, a programmer I met on an air force project. Ed was not keen on design.

Code is a tricky word. It is all of the human-readable symbols that make up a live program—not its design, but what programmers call the source: the symbols that when compiled or assembled can be executed on a computer. The symbols include things that would mean very little to a nonprogrammer: arguments and parameters, procedure calls, library references, macros, and a lot of other things that look more like names than instructions. Some people would include as code the variables that are changed by the program's logical and arithmetic operations; some would not. Some people would include as code the comments that describe the operations and the variables; some would not. "They are not code, because they are not executed by the computer." Nevertheless, all symbols represent programmer work. Harry would say that when someone asks you about your code, it's a good idea to clarify what he means, especially if he's your manager asking how much code you can write in a month.

Software managers like to count code. Lines of code are one of the benchmarks for estimating the size, cost, and duration of a software project. E. F. Schumacher wrote in *Small Is Beautiful* that "to undertake to measure the immeasurable is absurd and constitutes but an elaborate method of moving from preconceived notions to foregone conclusions." He was not thinking about computer programs, but his remark could be applied to software. We can measure lines of code. But we cannot measure the relationship between logical complexity and semantic correctness. Yet, when it comes to our dependence on and trust of automation, this is the relationship that counts the most.

Industrial programmers abhor the line of code. When managers speak of it, programmers quicken their step. Most of them know that the line of code is as central to the meaning of a program as the period is to the meaning of Tolstoy's *Anna Karenina*.

Still, the size of a program is important. We sell programs. We want to know how much they cost to write. We produce programs by writing symbols, so it would make sense to measure symbols. Yet the line of code, the programming statement, is ambiguous. In the 1970s, systems analysts and programmers developed algorithms using A Programming Language, or APL. It was a neat trick to see if you could write an entire algorithm, complete with array operations and matrix multiplication, in one line of code—just for the fun of doing it. The same algorithm written in FORTRAN, parsed into procedures, might take 300 lines of code.

Maurice Halstead, one of the early programming theorists, wrote a book about counting code, *Elements of Software Science*. He writes that there is a logarithmic relationship between the number of operators and operands—the variables—in an assembly language program and its textual size. His ideas seem less significant to me than the title of his book. Apparently, he felt that counting code is more of a science than writing it.

The line of code can become *very* ambiguous.

Computer systems are like biological systems. They can be adapted to specific environments without changing their structure. One set of programs can be written for many potential situations. How is this done? Programs do not simply modify values—changing a 3 to a 4, for example; they modify them under certain conditions. The conditions also involve values. Like any values, they are specified in variables, records, and files. One can change the behavior of a program by modifying the *condition* values. For example, a program might specify: if $X<n$ then "FIRE THE MISSILE." Suppose the variable n represents the number of kilometers from a friendly aircraft to a hostile aircraft. In one environment, n might be set to 4; in another, to 20. The same principle is at work when you set up your personal computer to display the text of one file in Times New Roman and the text of another in Algerian. You are supplying the n.

On the 9020 System we gave the condition values a name: *adaptation.* Programmers work hard at figuring out when and how to apply adaptation. But clams come by it naturally. Here is an example. All clams eject their larvae into the water. The larvae can then fasten themselves to a passing fish, invade its gills and, there, develop. Most clam larvae come with hooks, so they can grab hold. For some reason, the larvae of the Lampsilis, a freshwater clam, have no hooks. Sprayed into the backwater, the larvae would just glance off and fall unrequited to the bed. They need special help. The help comes from the Lampsilis itself. Remarkable as it sounds, the Lampsilis has a fake fish sticking out of its rear. It looks so real that you would mistake it for a fish if you were snorkeling in the area. The fake fish flops around like a guppy. It even has an eye. For sure, fish think it's a fish, because they come around in swarms. Then the Lampsilis can let go of its young. There is a good chance that they will be swallowed and make it to the gills through the digestive system—without hooks.

The Lampsilis accommodates to local circumstances. Its phony fish permits functional diversity without changing its fundamental (clam) structure. Adapting computer systems to a particular environment is not too different.

The 9020 System has one set of logical and arithmetic operators, no more and no fewer than needed for a single air route traffic control center. Yet the system supports 20 centers, each with different airspace, different radar coverage, and different configurations. Adapting one set of operators to 20 places is done with a trick, like that used by the Lampsilis. The programmers attach a unique set of condition values to the back of the operators to oblige the peculiarities of each site.

Implementing adaptation during the development of the 9020 System required that an adaptation compiler be written. There were too many sites and too many condition values to be specified manually. Unfortunately, the project schedule put the completion of the adaptation compiler first. But writing a program to produce values whose operators have not yet been invented is impossible. How do you write a compiler to produce the names of airway fixes when the logic describing airway operations is still a matter of argument? The task fell to a succession of managers who crumbled under its paradoxical weight. The last succeeded, not because he understood where his predecessors had failed but because enough time had elapsed to clarify the near-final form of the system. The bulk of the programs had been written; the operators were known. In the end, a miracle happened. In the case of the thousands of adaptable programming statements, two different programming organizations, working in parallel, created different parts of what amounts to a single computer instruction. One group wrote the operators, the if X< ... then. ... The other wrote the compiler that generated all of the n's. So dozens of programmers, reporting through two different management chains, collaborated to create thousands of statements like this one: if X<n then "HANDOFF THE AIRPLANE."

Miracles are not without problems. In 1984, during the development of the Host Computer System, in which the 9020 software was recoded to run on a 3083 computer, some of the programmers developed a rash that was never fully explained. I think it was caused by adaptation.

It turns out that, in 1965, the 9020 programmers also used adaptation to specify record lengths, indexes, and pointers—condition values, not for the air traffic control environment but for the programs. Thus, some of the condition values were not simple values, like 20, but complex psuedo-operators, like a pointer to the location of X. (The great mathematician John von Neumann cited this as one of the most powerful properties of the stored computer program: that the program—its operators, variables, and values—is a value as well and can therefore modify itself. He asserted that this would enable programs to learn as they ran on.)

In the example, the statement if X<n then "HANDOFF THE AIRPLANE" becomes much more complicated: if (p->X)<n then "HANDOFF THE AIRPLANE." Not only is the n in the original example imported from a file generated off-line by a separate organization, but p, the pointer to X, is as well.

Two decades later, on the Host Computer System, the young programmers hired for the project, and some of the older programmers who had developed the original 9020 code, tripped over this complexity. Bugs showed up in the air traffic control applications that could be fixed only by changing the adaptation compiler.

At the time, Harry wrote: "If a large computer system lasts long enough, there's a chance, albeit slim, that some of the people who created it and were changed by it might come around again, like in a dream, to see what they did. Then they might notice how they smashed through uncountable dependencies that traverse, not just huge structural, dynamic, lexical, and organizational domains sprawled across the planet, but a wide historical domain. How they managed to pull this off only to discover that values changed in 1984 can perturb the instructions to which they were first bound in 1969, and thus wreck airplanes."

Harry was wrong about one thing: the 9020 System has not wrecked any planes. According to the safety records, the programs are far less of a risk than the pilots and the airplanes. No incidents have been blamed on loops, even those bound by parameters imported from adaptation.

Less than two years after the completion of the Host Computer System, in 1988, the conundrum of adaptation approached the absurd on the FAA's Advanced Automation System. Adaptation was to be used to control the new 20" × 20" air traffic controller displays. The principle was the same. One set of logical and arithmetic operators would be written to manage the displays. But the characteristics of the displays—the colors, font sizes, windows, and so on—could vary by site, by air traffic control position, by individual controller.

The characteristics would be adapted. A strong case was made that this would reduce the number of lines of code in the display manager. But the lines of code *not* counted were legion. They included the language created to define the display adaptation, the adaptation compiler, and the code to link the adaptation to the display manager code. In fact, the total number of lines of code became enormous, because in this case the adaptable condition values were not simple values, not even simple operators like the pointers used on the 9020 System, but entire programs. Thus, a typical display manager statement might look this way: if X<n then "DISPLAY DATA BLOCK." But n could be a program of programs (if Z>Y and A=B then loop on G until . . .), all generated by a custom-built adaptation compiler staffed by an organization larger than that of the entire Host Computer System project. The interdependencies within one old-fashioned statement were stupefying.

The design and implementation of the display manager and its adaptation lumbered on for years, suffering from the same paradoxical Who Goes First? syndrome that infected the 9020 System project. As the complexity grew, the case that the adaptable approach would yield fewer lines of code grew louder. Eventually, softer voices prevailed. A new team was brought on. In increments, they reengineered the software, eliminating most of the adaptation. (Had von Neumann lived, he would have called us quitters.) The entire episode spanned years, and it added years to the project. It contributed mightily to the project's arabesque nature.

THE LIMITS OF SOFTWARE ARE NEVER MORE OBVIOUS THAN IN ITS TESTING

SOFTWARE SYSTEMS ARE BEYOND DISCRETE *AND* STATISTICAL ANALYSIS

A SINGLE INCORRECT STATE—OUT OF TWO TO THE TRILLIONTH STATES—CAN DOWN A ROCKET: TO FIND SUCH A FAULT IN A SOFTWARE SYSTEM WOULD REQUIRE A HUNDRED GENERATIONS OF PROGRAMMERS—BUT AFTER THE FIRST FAILURE IS FOUND AND FIXED, ALL BETS ARE OFF: THEY WOULDN'T BE TESTING THE SAME SYSTEM ANYMORE

WE CAN DESIGN AND BUILD FAIL-SAFE SYSTEMS, BUT CAN WE KNOW WE DID?

Journal Entry 48:

I've been following the Year 2000 problem for some time. It will cost us—what?—a trillion dollars. That's more than Charles Keating cost us when he ruined the savings and loan business.

It seems to me this is a testing problem more than anything else. One thing I've learned is that no system is free of faults. You cannot find them all. So get ready.

The same holds true for all symbol systems. In pharmacology, we test drugs on rats and cats, then on human beings, until we're satisfied they work, and that when they don't (not if, but when), the losses will be small. We cover our tracks by publishing warnings. Nevertheless, 100,000 people die each year from drugs. Not from overdoses or interactions with other drugs, just from taking them. "Life is a risk!" the technologists say, dragging out the more-good-than-harm argument.

I tested a lot of software. Big systems. I liked finding other people's problems, like a detective. You glare at the weaknesses in others, never your own.

I never ran a test that didn't find at least one failure—not only is the software impure, but so are the requirements specifications. And every time we fix the software, there is a 10 percent chance—according to my anecdotal studies!—we'll inject another fault. Those are the hardest to find: the faults that result from trying to get rid of them. It's a little like your three-year-old kid's DNA getting damaged from secondhand smoke. Forty years later, the genetic program finally fails and the doctor says: "I'm sorry; it's what we call type oat cell. Make arrangements."

6

· · ·

TESTING COMPUTER SYSTEMS

All the reindeer flying about the world should be
checked carefully for signs of fatigue.
— NEVIL SHUTE, *No Highway*

The meat of a computer system is the software. Given the nature of computer programs, abstract, complex beyond knowing, and the nature of programming, haphazard and idiosyncratic, largely the issue of independent young minds, you would think that testing would be given the highest priority. It isn't. Programmers are trained, if they are trained at all, to invent and translate algorithms to run on computers. There is a good deal of fun in this, and a lot more satisfaction when the results appear to be good. I say "appear" because, often, at the first sign of success, victory is claimed.

Many programmers do an adequate job of testing the logic of a single module. But testing an entire system is another matter. Once a module is absorbed into the mass of programs, running as part of the real world, the nature of testing changes.

Herbert Simon, the Nobel Prize–winning economist and one of the godfathers of artificial intelligence, writes that there are three kinds of systems: (1) linear—those that can be modeled predictably using discrete data; (2) nonlinear and predictable—those that can be modeled statistically; and (3) nonlinear but unpredictable—those that can't be modeled easily or modeled at all. Even modest computer systems fall into the third category. Not easily characterized, they are not easily tested. It is beyond practicality to test every state, every possible value set under every possible condition, and yet a fault in a single operation can, and has, destroyed rockets. Compounding the problem is this: Programmers are not trained in the natural sciences. The scientific method is not part of their curriculum. The men and women who are called upon to test computer systems know little, if anything, about running a simple experiment.

The Year 2000 problem is now consuming much of the First and the Fifth Worlds. The worst part of the problem is that success depends so much on testing and inspection. Testing is not what programmers like to do; they like to convert algorithms into computer programs and watch them run on the computer, hopefully the first time. Finding and fixing the bug is a matter of painstaking verification, of building test plans and test cases and reading designs and code and test data and dumps, as we once called them. There are companies that have used the situation to invent algorithms and programs to automate the work (which is often the first thing that occurs to a programmer or a programming organization: how can we turn this into a problem we can solve by writing code?); but by and large the work will not be the fun stuff. It will require persistence, the sort that marks the souls of archaeologists and gumshoes like Sam Spade—hour upon hour of digging for clues, vigilance, and patience, the kind that comes from not finding answers the first time, or the tenth.

Year 2000 programmers are being paid a lot of money for this dirty work, and for good reason. If we fail to find and fix all instances of the bug, the results are unpredictable—all but one. The *Washington Post* recently published an article on the panic that is already spreading. (The article ran on December 7, 1998, the anniversary of the attack on Pearl Harbor. Having read the *Post* for many years, I am certain this was not accidental.) The *Post* states that "the bug has been a rallying point for all manner of subcultures, from the Deep Ecology hippies to consciousness-raising spiritualists to apocalyptic fundamentalists to gun-toting militia organizers."

The government is spending billions of dollars to correct the shortsightedness, the *Post* reports: the "Internet acronym of the moment is TEOTWAWKI, The End Of The World As We Know It." But not only the extremists are beginning to act; the middle-of-the-roaders are as well. Just as regular folks built bomb shelters in the 1950s and 1960s to add life time to a planet white with nuclear snow, regular folks are now storing large caches of food, water, toilet paper, clothing, and, of course, the American twinship: sacred literature and ammo. One man who agreed to be interviewed for the piece was quoted: "When you first hear about it, most people are in total denial. They can't believe that Bill Gates won't come up with a magic bullet." (That the general population believes that Bill Gates has the answers to our programming problems is more frightening than the rollover of the millennium.)

I have a good feel for what it is like to spend hours and hours just testing. I tested the 9020 System relentlessly for four years. Testing on that scale reminded me of raking leaves on a windy day. As a kid, I liked jumping into piles of leaves, but I hated raking them. My father insisted I help him. But I never saw the sense in it. The leaves looked perfectly fine on the lawn. If system failures were leaves, I filled dozens of baskets testing the 9020 software. But I watched others blow away. I pinned some down later, but there were always more. I learned that I couldn't find all of them. It would be like finding all the fallen leaves in Vermont.

What I didn't know then was that I didn't know what I was doing. I was writing and running tests as if the system were linear and predictable. I ran the same tests with the same inputs over and over until I found no more failures. Testing this way is like counting drops to measure the behavior of a waterfall.

Luckily, I was surrounded by more savvy engineers and programmers. They tested the system from a dozen angles, at the FAA's insistence. There were tests to stress the system's capacity; ergonomic tests; tests for each air traffic control situation, for each type of controller input and output; equipment tests; throughput tests; adaptation tests; clock tests; tests for the engineering position; interface tests; tests using field adaptation; intersystem tests, between the 9020 (en route) System and the ARTS terminal system; tests with simulated radar; tests with live radar; tests to find failures in the failure recovery hardware and software; tests to verify that error messages were easy to understand and consistently formatted; tests using random inputs to measure behavior statistically—getting at the nonlinear and predictable aspect of the system; tests of the software that builds the system, of the software that records the data used to analyze the tests, of the test harness, and of the tests themselves. The tests were run under as many different conditions as time allowed. The FAA demands safety; it is their mission. Lives are at stake. There would be no letting the users discover the failures.

John, with whom I teach software engineering management at Johns Hopkins University, worked on NASA's Space Shuttle System. The testing of that system was (and is) as comprehensive as the testing of the 9020 System. But the approach used to test the shuttle system is different: it is tested using a simulator. John tells the class that as much software was written to develop the simulator as was written for the mission itself. The objective of the simulator was to create an environment in the laboratory as close to the real world as possible. The simulator models the unlikely as well as the likely situations; and it models all of the interfaces.

The simulator is a closed system. As such, it is far more predictable and reliable than the environment it is simulating. It is also a feedback system. Mechanisms to stimulate the space shuttle software and return responses are built in. Thousands of test cases can be run predictably in a week instead of hundreds. So the hunt for failures is intensified and the probability of ruin is reduced. (The probability of a failure in a computer system is never zero. There are always failures—if not evident, then latent.)

The simulator software had to be tested as thoroughly as the software it was built to test. A fault in the simulator would cause the worst kind of problem, what computer analysts call a Byzantine failure. Byzantine failures are like traitors in a family. The one you trust the most to tell you the truth lies. There is always a risk this will happen.

NASA was willing to spend the millions of dollars and the time to build the simulator for the same reason the FAA invests so heavily in testing: safety. As John says, "You just don't want the astronauts debugging." But not many projects work this way. Often a covenant is made early in a project's life cycle: We will discover no failures as soon as possible. There is good reason for this. First, discovering a failure is disappointing, and then there is the pressure from above not to find them. Everyone wants the software out the door. On government-sponsored projects, promises have been made to Congress. In the commercial field, competition drives businesses to release software early. A product announcement alone can drive up stock prices, and the sooner the better. Next to the price of a share, failures are annoying, yes, but we can live with them.

Two of the great questions in developing computer systems are (1) When do we stop testing? and (2) At any point during testing, how far along are we? The second question cannot be answered until the first one has been answered. The first question can be answered by fiat. The product is due out on September 1, so we have to be done by then. Or we have $4 million budgeted for testing. We're done when the money runs out. But these answers beg another question: How good is the system when we stop? Set aside politics and economics, and consider science. Assume we can define what we mean by *good*. If we can define it and quantify it, we are well on our way to knowing when to stop, and how long it will take to get there.

On the Host Computer System project the programming team, managers and staff, defined the good, at least as they saw it. For example: When it finally arrives, is the system dependable? Does the system do what it was intended to do? Is it easy to use and maintain? Does it leave room for growth? Is it compatible with the system it is replacing? Does it recover from failures without compromising service? Is it responsive?

Before they measured these parameters (and others), they modeled them. With the FAA, they defined an acceptable range of values for each. Some were specified in the system's requirements document. They projected the system's performance over time with respect to the acceptable values. The result was a set of curves like those you would see in boardrooms, where sales managers show the projected growth in revenues.

A critical parameter in the development of any system is the discovery rate of software failures, especially during system testing. To draw a projected failure discovery curve for a system in the making is difficult, even if historical data are available. On the Host project the programming team had very little historical data. But they had an idea of what the discovery curve would look like. Defect discovery data have been tracked for years in the automotive industry. Analysts had studied their insertion and discovery from the piece-part, through the assembly with other parts, to the finished product. And someone somewhere, maybe a dozen someones in a dozen places simultaneously, began to collect data on software projects. They noticed trends. They noticed that, during a system's development, the discovery rate of software failures increases slowly but steadily, then accelerates steeply to a graceful peak. The graph looks like a beginner's ski slope. But then the corner is turned and the discovery rate angles downward sharply in what mathematicians would call an exponential decay. The discovery rate never goes to zero but levels off.

On the Host project, not one but two projections were made: a best case and a worst case. These were based on the size of the software, its complexity, the schedule, the number of test hours, and the laboratories available. The curves bound the course of progress. Each week, the number of software failures discovered in the laboratory was plotted and compared with the model. Every month the model was calibrated. Sometimes more failures than expected were found; sometimes fewer. Either way, the team wanted to make sure they were not finding too few because the testing was inadequate. If they were finding more than expected, they dug into the reasons. Programming teams examined the methods they were using. Sometimes important steps had been skipped; sometimes it was a matter of inadequate training; sometimes the code was more complicated than anticipated. Regardless, action was taken to improve.

The team learned that statistics are not enough. The *kind* of failures, correlated with their frequency, gives a clearer picture of the health of the system. The team categorized failures, from critical to modest. In psychology, periodic hallucinations are more alarming than a persistent rash. So, near the end of testing, if only 10 failures are found per month but they all crash the system, you are farther behind, much farther behind, than if you had found 50 instances of a misspelled error message.

This technique was used for all of the system performance parameters. It paid off. The Host project was completed on schedule and under budget, and it has supported air traffic control dependably for a dozen years. The good was achieved, I believe, because, at any point in time, the entire project team knew the health of the system. They knew how much true progress was being made, how much bona fide product was being produced with respect to the schedule and the budget.

There is still no simple answer to the two great questions. You can test forever and not find all of the failures. Of one thing I am sure, though: You have to be looking for them. Setting out to demonstrate their absence will, sooner or later, distort the nature of testing.

There may be other avenues to constrain the task, to test fully, but not indefinitely. Harry believed that systems should be tested only as they will be used. The system is artificial without people in it, he would say: "I wouldn't know what to call the computers and their programs without people using them. But it's not a system. The people, after all, help shape a system's boundaries, adjust its form. Machines, computer programs, and humans must reconcile."

Systems are like jaguars or kingfishers. They do well in some habitats and not in others. If I were to lift the 9020 System from its familiar den, plop it down somewhere else, and ask it to flex some of its seldom-used muscles, it would wince, even break. The green kingfisher seldom moves far from southern Texas. You could say it likes it there. Or, maybe if it left, it would risk extinction. Its "there" is part of its self. It is comfortable perched on the banks of the slow-moving Texas backwaters hunting small river fish. On land it loses something. Quite fit to walk, it is unpracticed at it. The bird waddles around as if on Thorazine.

Harry may be right. Large computer systems are built far beyond the regular thread of their daily use. Each time we change them, hike up their level of automation, we put in a little extra here and there, just in case they might have to walk on water. They seldom try. But then, once in a great while, something odd happens, something unanticipated, like a hot day in January, and you're sorry you didn't test everything. As if you could.

SOFTWARE MANAGERS USING ENGINEERING METHODS CAN OVERCOME THE BIOLOGICAL NATURE OF PROGRAMMING

SOFTWARE MANAGERS SHOULD SUFFER THE BIOLOGY OF PROGRAMMING—FOR MORE THAN A YEAR OR TWO

Journal Entry 50:

I became a software manager after only a few years of programming. Looking back, I feel cheated. It wasn't enough. I skipped shift work and the rigors of configuration control and system integration, when entire modules were missing from the build list, and I would have had to call people in the middle of the night.

I learned, secondhand, that the development of a software manager is like that of any human: you can't skip steps. If you do, your insight and ability to cope will have been arrested, and you will, thereafter, only limp along among the walking wounded.

Supervision cannot overcome the lack of precise planning. But even planning cannot overcome the facts: software functions do not come to life until the very end of their development and testing. It isn't so much a matter of not taking credit for work as yet unfulfilled—which is in itself noble and courageous—but of giving leeway for it. As Norman Augustine has said, successful managers build in reserves. In programming, this is not enough. Managers must find the middle ground between the severity of the classical production cycle and the unfathomable, the transfer of an individual's logical thinking, through symbols, to machines that run at near the speed of light.

I wonder how many others have had a similar experience: working among software managers who were promoted in the short run—before the final tally, the feedback from the field on how well the software fits into the procedures of the real world, how well it forgives our mistakes, how well it supports other programs that may run atop it five years hence—and, having had enough, then left to find another job and a promotion, or started their own consulting firms? Why waste precious time seeing things through?

7

. . .

THE IMPOSSIBLE PROFESSION

*For the real revolution in medicine, which set the
stage for antibiotics and whatever else we have in
the way of effective therapy today, had already
occurred one hundred years before penicillin. It did
not begin with the introduction of science into
medicine. That came years later. Like a good many
revolutions, this one began with the destruction of
dogma. It was discovered, sometime in the 1830s,
that the greater part of medicine was nonsense.*
— LEWIS THOMAS, *The Medusa and the Snail*

A paragraph like this may someday be written about programming.
Hopefully, it will be followed by an entry that would read . . . but the
best of the early programming managers followed the lead of turn-of-
the-century American physicians. They filled their notebooks and
journals with times, places, personal histories, symptoms, survival
rates, the basic readings from a few reliable instruments. They
needed all the help they could get to make diagnoses, suggest reme-
dies, and prepare the way for those who would follow.

Roper is such a manager. A software manager for more than thirty years, he collects data as if he were doing research. He is. Not satisfied to lead projects, he wants to learn and pass on what he has learned. He would not agree with Harlan Mills, who liked to say we have not yet discovered the right triangle in programming. Roper believes that there is no right triangle to be discovered. "I can do nothing to change the nature of software," he says. "It's more like writing than bridge-building. I just want to manage it as if it were bridge-building."

Roper's credenza is filled with data from the many projects he has managed—what programs were written and why, according to this or that method of design, for which requirements, in how many increments, by how many programmers, using which methods, under what sort of contract, for how much money, using which languages, running on which computers. There are data about the size of programs and how they were changed. There are data about faults and failures: when they were injected; when they were found and how—by inspection, by testing; their effect on modules; and on and on. Stuck away amid the thick piles of paper are charts and graphs that correlate the figures any number of ways. His notebooks are filled with them.

Roper refuses to draw conclusions. The size of the sample is too small, he says. "One project can last five or ten years. And there are too many intangibles. Let's take the matter of success. What is success? Making money? Push-button wars? Automating schools? Then there are the programmers and the managers and their styles, changing technology and techniques, the ebb and flow of commitment, culture, corporations, governments, and the relationships between them. You decide. Come to think of it, if we pass on enough data, maybe our great-grandchildren could tender a verdict. Maybe they will discover that computer systems aren't worth studying. Or maybe that they shouldn't have been built in the first place."

One reason Roper keeps the data around is that he's afraid to let go of it. He told me, "If it's gone, people won't believe me. Our recall of projects is selective. Myths grow up around them. Maybe things didn't happen a certain way, maybe they did. Maybe some things didn't happen at all! I read about successful projects and I wonder, were they successful or were they just declared successful?"

Roper knows about truth and memory, desire and belief. He is an idealist of the most fervent sort: at times, his views of how the world *should be* get mixed in with, or overshadow, how it *is*. So, when asked if the company gives out awards, he might well say no. Whether or not it does is unimportant. Roper, a Marxist at heart, believes the company should not give out awards. So, in his mind, it doesn't.

Roper told me what happened to him in Jacksonville, debugging the 9020 System. He was working third shift for over a year, 16 hours a day sometimes, straight through sometimes. In the middle of the night there were usually no operators around. For a couple of hours at least, programmers were on their own. One week the programmer with computer time right before Roper caught his eye. Roper said she stood "maybe five feet eight." "She always wore white pants and a white blouse and no jewelry. She had hair the color of sunrise and her face was as white as her clothes." Roper's computer time started at 3 A.M., right after "the Irish girl," as he called her. She would run her job and leave after 45 minutes. "After she ran, I had trouble running my tests. The system would do crazy things." He would reload and run diagnostics. Everything seemed normal, but then the system would crash. "She had done something. What bothered me most was the lights on the 9020 panel." There were three rows, one for each processor, 32 bits long. Normally, after a run, one row was off, or maybe two, or all three, or one row had a well-worn pattern programmers recognized as the computer waiting for work. But the lights at 2:45 A.M. always spelled out what looked to Roper like "eel."

He wanted to know why "eel." He tried to work the problem inside out. What must be going on in the 9020 to spell out "eel" on the instruction address registers? He'd take dumps of low storage as soon as he got on, to trace through the protected areas where things start or they don't start at all. He found nothing. Those lights just don't come on, he told me. Roper looked up everything he could find about eels: where they lived, in what part of the ocean, where people ate them, everything. He should have been sleeping during the day, but instead he was in the library.

The next week she was gone. The first chance he got, Roper asked Joe about her. Joe was the oldest and best computer operator and he knew everybody. Joe said he heard that there was a programmer on site who used to leave the lights in a funny way after each run. But he wasn't sure. One of the other guys who had retired told him. It was a woman, and all he knew was that she'd lost her husband in Vietnam. The guy thought his name was Ed.

"It wasn't 'eel'; it was 'ed'!"

Joe said the joke was that her dead husband was in the 9020 and he was communicating with her.

"Some joke!"

Then Roper told Joe that he saw it happen and he saw her. He went on for ten minutes. Joe just looked at him in that funny way he looked at IBM programmers who thought they walked on water. "Hey man, that story's been around for years."

Roper went on. "She must have been Irish. I never saw anyone like her."

Joe looked at him and just laughed. "How long you been on third shift? The 'ed' girl was Asian and besides, . . . well, I heard she died. Cancer or something."

THE SECRET TO MANAGING SOFTWARE

The British writer Alistair Cooke claims golf was discovered by the Scots to instill Calvinism in their youth: "Golf was just what the Scottish character had been seeking for centuries; namely, a method of self-torture, disguised as a game." There may be something to that.

About forty or fifty years ago, it was said that Ben Hogan had discovered the secret to hitting perfect golf shots. Arguably, Hogan was the finest ball striker who ever swung a club. But he would not share his secret. There was speculation that he did something tricky with his hands at the top of his backswing. No doubt, golfers the world over were trying everything. If they could find the secret, maybe they could play like Hogan.

Ben Hogan died in 1997. But he didn't take his secret with him. In his last years he acknowledged that there was indeed a secret. "It's in the dirt," he told a reporter courageous enough to ask him.

Learn the fundamentals and then practice them. The fundamentals of managing software are not hard to describe, nor are they hard to practice. If there is a secret, it is this. Superimpose onto the business of symbol writing the management practices of classical production, but allow for the eccentricities of the symbol writers.

To some degree, we cannot know what we cannot see. Therefore, we must define abstractions as if they were bumpers or pencils. Thus, we begin by defining products: each specification, each design, each procedure, each module, each subsystem, each function, each manual, and so on, throughout the life cycle. Merely declaring designs or modules as products is not enough; they must be made visible. They are made visible by inspection or by testing. These verification events, when laid out on a schedule, become milestones. Each milestone gives us the opportunity to *know*, to know that progress has been made, that the products do what we intended them to do. But when we look at them or use them, we know more than how good they are. We also know how much time and money we spent on them.

Progress cannot be tracked without first developing a plan: defining the products and all of the activities that go into making them; the schedule; the budgets. This must be done in detail and written down. Then products can be mapped to people, departments, and organizations, so that accountability can be fixed. Planning is a form of design. Good software managers are good designers. They must also have a bent for rigor. Undefined products, activities unaccounted for, optimistic milestones and budgets: any and all of these can set a plan that at best is risky and at worst will encourage imprecise, even deceptive, measurement.

Successful managers build in reserves: financial, schedule, and quality.

Financial reserves account for potential cost overruns, which can result from poor planning and poor execution, but also from the unforeseen, the risks. Good people leaving. Bad weather. Requirements changes. The list is long. Managers must know the skill and experience of the people who work or will work for them. They must know rates of production for the genus of functions and applications under development for each of the many activities, such as designing, coding, testing, writing manuals. (The variables embedded within *productivity* are legion. These are but a few: What programming languages will be used? How complex is the system being renovated or created? Are techniques and methods well understood and documented?) Engineering managers in all disciplines should understand the company's financial apparatus to some degree—the labor rates and how they are calculated, for example. How does writing and testing one line of code affect the bottom line? Perhaps we should subcontract some of the work to companies more expert and that operate less expensively—but without compromising the standards our company has set.

Establishing schedule reserves is no less complicated. Keen managers insist on fashioning dependency networks. Work can be done in sequence, in parallel, and concurrently—that is, task B can begin only after a portion of task A has been completed. Tasks are laid out in relation to one another and the resources they require, in terms of both their planned start and completion dates. (In general, no task should be defined that takes longer than a few weeks, say, from four to seven.) Then the network is studied. How early can we start task C if we overrun task B, upon whose completion C depends? How late can we start a task without compromising the entire schedule? Do we need the same people on task A and task C? And the same laboratories? Allowing for the unforeseen, how much risk can we tolerate? Reserves are built into the network as slack. A sound network is not brittle, so that each and every task must begin and end in perfect synchrony. A sound network sags a bit, enough to allow for changes in productivity, in requirements, and so on. This is called critical path management, and it has been around for much of the twentieth century.

Quality reserves are defined by modeling or projecting the performance of the product or system as it is being developed and integrated, in terms of a best and worst case. Performance means all properties of the system that make up its intrinsic and perceived quality, such as response times, failure rates, meaningful error messages, ease of use and repair. Permitting some variation on the journey to goodness does not mean compromising it. In the end, quality will be achieved. But more faults may be inadvertently injected into a module than anticipated. More failures may be discovered in June than predicted. Allowances should be made, and, along with them, recovery plans. The principles are roughly the same that underlie financial and schedule management.

Like a point in space, the earned value system, as it is sometimes called, joins the three quantities: the product and its quality, its cost, and the time to produce it. When it is planned and executed in earnest, managers can know for any product or combination of products that 20 percent of the work has been completed for 30 percent of the budget in 40 percent of the scheduled time. The example indicates that there may be a cost problem and a schedule problem. If the products were not well defined, or shortcuts were taken in evaluating them, a quality problem may exist as well.

We use an example at Johns Hopkins: Project X. The software development plan has been completed and inspected. Every product, every verification step, every method, has been recorded. Nothing has been left to the imagination. Templates have been created to ensure uniformity. The exit criteria, the conditions under which a product can be deemed complete at each stage of its development, carry Talmudic authority. Quality, time, and money have been pinned to each milestone. Milestones are frequent.

A programmer completes the testing of a single procedure. He reports that his milestone has been met. He has exceeded the budget and the schedule allocated for this activity, but not by much. The earned value is calculated. Later in the week, the programmer's manager overhears the programmer tell a colleague that he will have to come in over the weekend to fix the seven or eight bugs he found testing his procedure. He's not sure if he has time to retest the procedure. He's supposed to start another task on Monday.

The milestone has not been met after all. The exit criterion read "no bugs." The earned value is in question.

Imagine this happening here and there, now and again, across hundreds, perhaps thousands, of procedures and modules and files and test data and documents, over the course of a years-long project. Now imagine this: There is no software development plan. Methods are not prescribed. Months pass between milestones. Costs are not correlated to products and schedules. Managers are not held accountable. Then it is not hard to imagine this: as one Secretary of the Navy put it, "How did a $500 million project get years behind in one month?"

Roper likes to talk about the antimanagers. That's what he calls managers who know the secret but don't like it very much. They want plenty of time and money; nice, committed people working for them; and no risks. They often complain that they cannot do their job. "You have to like challenges to enjoy management," says Roper. "With all the time and money in the world, people won't even try. So then what is management?"

He is right, of course. We all need the noose tightened—in a cordial way. The pope was on Michelangelo's back every day. Dostoyevsky wrote *Crime and Punishment* as a serial, two weeks at a time. Without deadlines, who knows what they would have been doing? Michelangelo chasing after his students? Dostoyevsky gambling his family away?

Admittedly, managing software can become unbearable, like grief. Roper told me about a small California company that dispensed with it altogether. Plans and controls were proving too much for the programmers, who threatened to walk out. The job was too important to allow this to happen. They were writing programs to assimilate data on neurological disorders such as Parkinson's disease and multiple sclerosis. So the company phased out leadership and introduced large decision-making boards and paper directives. Over time, the lack of accountability reduced friction. Programmer morale soared. The whole arrangement took on the appearance of a system, like a system of pulleys and levers. There were advantages, Roper pointed out. It empowered people. Although I have never been to one, I suppose the project resembled a New England town meeting, where everyone votes on how much to spend on snow removal and sanding for the coming year. I wonder, if systems could think and feel, how would this system view the atrophy of a second-line manager? The project failed.

An IBM manager, Alan Scherr, decided to find out if you could set tough schedules and budgets and make them. He and a cadre of managers took over a number of projects that were overdue, over budget, or both. Then he wrote about it. Scherr would only take on projects that agreed to his rules, which were simple: the staff must commit to beating the schedule, lowering costs, and improving the quality of the products, and they could not work overtime.

The outcome was surprising. All the projects turned around. Some completed with better results than expected. Scherr's report does not mention technical methods, perhaps because they aren't important after all. What *is* important is that workers' backs were put to the wall, so they could change nothing but themselves. As long as human beings are encouraged to maintain the status quo, and there are no significant consequences, they will merely endure. But if they find themselves beyond their tolerance for discomfort, they will seek help. They will bottom out.

On Scherr's projects, the status quo was not permitted. This, no doubt, unhinged many of the staff's psychological props. Everyone bottomed out. Within weeks, a young programmer who never read code pored over it. An unusually shy tester opened up at a meeting. A dominating manager listened. A man afraid to go home and face his children left work on time. A systems engineer stood up to his manager for the first time. A young woman, reluctant to give talks, gave one. A tense, obsessive architect stopped talking for a while. An inveterate meeting-goer wrote down a schedule. A reticent programmer led. A maverick sought help; a careerist gave it to him. A programmer found a bug and was comforted. A sense of purpose reigned. Details ran like blood, but the big picture was not lost. Everyone taught everyone else. No one gave up.

Despite the successes, work on those projects could not have been much fun. When the staff said good-bye to the management team, it must have been with glee. Afterward, they could revert to blaming others, working mindless overtime, complaining, showing off, playing up, squandering talent. They could, once again, be themselves and breathe easy. But then, after a long while, they might remember that they once did something extraordinary.

PROFESSIONALISM: DISCIPLINE AS ART
DEATH PENALTY HAS LITTLE EFFECT ON LIFE EXPECTANCY

Journal Entry 52:

Do you wonder why some great college athletes never make it in the pros? My guess is that they get by on talent alone in the school ranks. They lack the commitment that spurs the drive that drives the hours of practice and loyalty to getting a job done, the *present* job, without being distracted by where-can-I-go-from-here.

In football, how many highly touted collegiate running backs are willing to block for someone else? In the late 1990s, I saw Herschel Walker, one of the most prolific backs in football history, then at the age of 37, relegated to special teams—kickoffs and punt returns—and spot assignments from scrimmage, catch up to and tackle a 22-year-old speed merchant who had intercepted a pass just before he reached the end zone. Walker made up 20 yards in seconds. (He had once run the hundred in 9.3 seconds.) He seemed to come out of nowhere, passing other players as if they were standing still. That day, he looked as if he were running the hundred in 9 seconds flat, and he may well have—except no one was timing him—with 20 lbs. of equipment on him. What could have inspired such desire? He was by then a millionaire, and he surely was well known, at least in athletic circles. Self respect? Commitment? Professionalism! Maybe they are all entwined. I don't know. But when I feel like quitting, I think about Herschel Walker in the autumn.

As difficult and frustrating as they are, software projects are also inspiriting. Once joined, engineers, programmers, testers, managers, and specialists set their jaws, as if this were the last project on Earth. There are rough spots, as in any society, but, looking back, I am proud and happy when I remember the U.S. space program and the other projects in which I played a part, however small. As Richard Wilbur puts it in his poem "The Writer," recalling his daughter helping a dazed starling escape from the confines of her attic room, "It is always a matter, my darling, of life or death, as I had forgotten."

8

· · ·

LIFE ON THE PROJECT

*It is almost eight years since I retired from the water-
front, but in my dreams I still load and unload ships.*
— ERIC HOFFER, *Before the Sabbath*

Computer systems are fun to imagine but awful to build. When I
look back at projects and the programmers who worked on them, I
think of the soldiers at Agincourt heaving their broad swords in the
mud for hours, then sinking in exhaustion, one atop the other.

When a project begins, expectations are high. Giddiness is in
the air. There is usually an early success: the demonstration of a simple function, perhaps. Awards are given. Expectations rise. But the
next increment, or the next, founders. A recovery plan is put in
place. More people are brought in. Milestones begin to slide.
Nevertheless, optimism prevails. Then there is a turning point. Just
about everyone loses interest in the design and debugging takes over.
With months or years to go, every day becomes the last day; every
hour, the last hour. Tiger teams are created. Daily meetings are
held. The labs are in use 24 hours a day. More software is written.

Functions that once worked no longer work. Unforeseen software tools needed for testing and debugging are written and rushed to the front. The system is too complicated. The programmers ask, How did we get into this? If the system is being written for a government agency, the contractor begs for relief, or demands it. The agency responds by asking for more function. Managers are replaced. Programmers leave. The project heaves and slogs on.

In the 1970s I worked on a very successful project, one of the great feats of diligence in the early years. As systems go, it wasn't large or complex. Digital photographs of Earth taken from the Landsat satellite had to be modified before they could be developed. Programs were written to correct distortions in the image caused by Earth's curvature and the camera.

A special computer was built for the project: an array processor. The computer came with two power supplies: one for the fan and one for the processor. Every night an engineer powered off the computer. The processor was to be powered off first, then the fan. One night someone powered off the fan and left the processor running, and the computer melted. It became known as the crispy critter. This was a major setback, especially because months earlier the project had overrun its entire budget in one unlucky afternoon, when it was learned that a specially built disk controller would cost $2 million instead of the estimated $200,000.

Not long after the meltdown, a programming manager broke both his feet jumping off a garage and had to be replaced. He said he tripped, but no one believed him. He crossed several state borders to get away and fell into the Gulf of Mexico. Then a programmer who was working on the system diagnostics crossed over the yellow line on a back road and hit a car head on. The woman driving the other car was killed in an instant. The programmer kept coming to work, but he spoke to no one. I would pass his office from time to time. He sat like a board in his chair with his arms folded across his chest looking straight ahead. His mind was looping, someone said. A couple of months later, a young programmer drove her Corvette into the side of a stone barn beside a cornfield. She lingered for a few days before dying. From the looks of the tracks, the police said, she must have rehearsed. Afterward, programmers wouldn't touch her code. Maybe they felt it was sacred, or they were afraid of it, that it would somehow spread the terror and despair felt by its author.

Sometimes, though, the terror is a result of being separated from the code. A lead programmer on the project bought a trailer and lived in the parking lot at work so he could be near the code—not just his code, but all the code, and the libraries and macros and job control statements, and all the gear that ran them. He said he wanted to feel their cool rush around him. He would awaken suddenly at 2 A.M., thinking he forgot to clear a buffer, and pad across the parking lot in his thongs to the computer room, fire up the machines, and look at storage dumps. There he'd find his buffer cleared and he would breathe easier. But then he would find another bug. At 7 A.M. the operators would show up and ask if he'd been there all night. He said he didn't know, but wondered if the coffee was on.

The Strategic Air Command's Digital Network System, SACDIN, was another dreadful project that ended in a great system. It reminds me that the act of meeting ordinary, daily demands can transform itself into an extraordinary achievement—hundreds of people grinding out thousands of programs until it all works. In the end they buried our code in missile holes. I wrote a program to send the Emergency Action Message. The EAM sets nuclear missiles in motion. Afterward, if enough EAMs were sent, there would be no programming, only code. Unaffected by the nuclear winter, the programs would go on spinning. In time, they might terminate gracefully, just as designed.

There were obstacles on the SACDIN project. There are always obstacles. For example, one hot July day, a new cleaning crew showed up. Only the supervisor spoke some English, I was told later. The next morning we arrived at work and our listings were gone. There was no paper anywhere. Some mix-up about what was trash. The cleaning crew had cleared the offices.

The problem was that Ved, one of the project's key program-mers, had written his notes from a design inspection on his listing. We had no choice, he said; we must get the listing. By this time it was in the truck by the loading dock, along with hundreds of other listings. Four of us went to the dock. The truck was an 18-wheeler, big enough to live in. There was a hill of paper in the trailer. One of the programmers clambered up the right side, where it looked like firm footing. Mahlon, Ved's manager, went straight up the front to the top, to see if he could get at the back. Two of us just started in. Ved was not among us. He was back in his air-conditioned office, seeing if he could get by without the listing.

Around noon we broke for lunch. Someone had brought chicken salad sandwiches. We bolted them down and kept going. At around one o'clock I started thinking about what happened in 1967. That summer my friend Gary and I went to my fraternity house to shoot pool in the afternoons before work. It was closed for the sum-mer, but I had a key. It was hot as blazes in there, like the trailer. During the third or fourth week we smelled it: a rancid odor that seemed to be coming from the walls. The pool table was on the first floor in the middle of the house between the living room and the dining room, and next to Mrs. Peters's apartment. (Colleges employed housemothers in those days.) Gary was the first to say something: "There is something dead in here." We finished a game of eight ball and left. The next week, we went back. I had forgotten about the smell. When we opened the door, the air flattened us. The odor occupied your mouth and nose and gut like a living thing. "There is something dead in there, all right," I said as I shut the door. "It's not a pigeon, either." Gary said that it must be a dog. But how did it get in? I remembered that Mrs. Peters had told me she was going to Colorado for the summer. Suddenly I wasn't so sure. She was over 80 and forgetful. She smoked ferociously. After careful thought, we went around the side of the house. There was a window in the apartment bedroom. Gary hoisted me partway and I managed to get a foothold. The window wasn't locked, and I opened it somehow. Halfway through I was thinking about what I might find and about the stories passed down through our family about Gettysburg after the battle, how the stench of decaying horses and men and mules would not depart the Blue Ridge valley, that it stuck there like a pain in the lower back. I threw up on her oriental rug. Then I kicked open the bedroom door. Nothing. Then the bathroom. Nothing. I got more confident. "She's not in here!" I yelled. I went out the back, through the outside door, and saw Gary running up the street. I locked the house and went home. Weeks later, when school started and Mrs. Peters had returned, someone found the capons in the unplugged freezer behind the pantry. The fire department cleaned it out and buried it somewhere.

Not long after lunch Mahlon found Ved's listing. He emerged from the truck waving it triumphantly. By that time I could care less. He told me he'd take us out for lunch tomorrow. Barbecue, he said. "We need a better backup plan," I remarked.

There was no backup plan for the Landsat project manager. Lee was addicted to eating paper. He'd bring a tablet to meetings. Every fifteen minutes or so, you would hear a rip from down the table. At the beginning of the project he would tear a page into small pieces and stuff them into his mouth, incrementally. Later on, as the project's troubles deepened, he would devour entire sheets. Once, Lee's deputy had given him an important memo from NASA. Before a copy could be made, he had swallowed it. The deputy had to scramble a little, but he managed to get the agency to send it again. After the project ended I heard that Lee had changed his life. He took some time off, went to parks, and lived in tents. A few years passed and I ran into one of the project's engineers. He told me that he'd seen Lee at headquarters gnawing on a pencil. Lee told him that he wanted to get into politics next.

Sometimes projects never get started. A golfing buddy of mine, George, went to the Soviet Union to sell Gorbachev an air traffic control system. "Russia is a funny place. No one trusts anyone. People don't trust themselves. And they believe in their incompetence.

They're proud of it." On his first trip, George landed at the airport outside of Moscow. No one was there to meet him. After a couple of anxious hours, he phoned the hotel and got a cab. The cab ride took about an hour, with several stops along the way for no apparent reason. He checked in and called his hosts. One was a KGB officer who would be his translator. It took an hour before he got through to someone who spoke English. The man knew about George Hubbard—he worked for IBM and was expected from the United States. But he said George had not arrived yet. George said he *had* arrived. *He* was George. But the man was firm. People had gone to the airport and there was no George Hubbard; therefore, there was no George Hubbard. George explained that he had taken matters into his own hands. The man couldn't understand that. George Hubbard simply was not in the Soviet Union.

Later, toward evening, George heard a knock on his door and opened it. There stood a prostitute. She spoke a little English. She said she was part owner of the hotel, along with the desk clerk. She asked George if he wanted to have sex with her. George said no, but he was hungry and wanted something to eat. She demanded 15 American dollars anyway and told him about a restaurant. George paid her. There were two kinds of money in the Soviet Union, he said: "They go with the lines. Long lines mean rubles. Short lines are for people with Western currency, like dollars." George went to the restaurant, where he got a sandwich that looked like a mixture of Spam and fat, and a bowl of soup. "The soup was pretty good."

The next day he was contacted. Much of the time he was accompanied by several Soviet men, who, he said, are as burly as we imagine them to be: "They are very physical." George is stocky. He was an All-Big 8 football player in the 1950s. The Soviets liked his size and liked pounding him on the shoulders.

His hosts insisted that he drink shots of vodka at every meal. George rarely drinks. He faked it as much as he could. He poured vodka into the water, into the soup, into potted plants. Meals were also a time for singing—with gusto. One night his new friends asked

George to stand up and sing an American song. George said he couldn't sing and didn't know any songs. They insisted. He stumbled to his feet, half-drunk but still wary, and sputtered through "I've Been Workin' on the Railroad." They went wild.

Later that same night, on his way back to the hotel, he was mugged by gypsies. A woman tried to steal his wallet. He hit her in the mouth, which appalled him. The other gypsies laughed, and then everyone ran away, including George.

On his second visit, George was given a tour of Moscow. He was taken to factories. He toured museums. He was shown apartment buildings constructed under Stalin. They were all plain and gray—that is, all but one, which had an unusual facade over the front door. George asked about it. The KGB translator explained. Stalin visited the apartment complex once, just after it was built, and complained that the buildings were too drab. He wanted something more artistic—and soon. So a small scroll and a couple of columns were added to one of the buildings. A photograph was taken and hurried back to the tyrant, who seemed pleased.

George said there was no bookkeeping in the Soviet Union. No one knew how much anything cost. Things were just built. No one kept records. The Soviets had no idea how much a doorknob costs, much less an automated air traffic control system.

The highlight of his final trip was the meeting. The Soviets had been talking about it for several days. They were "real spun up about it." George asked a couple of times what was so funny. They said, "You'll see." When the big day arrived, the translator spilled the beans: "We don't know how to run a meeting." He let out a big laugh. "You'll see."

At around two in the afternoon, after a few vodkas, everyone strolled into a large studio room with a single table and some chairs around it. On the table were some glasses. The Soviets were already laughing. They sat down. George could sit at the end opposite the leader. For a few minutes nothing happened. Then the leader spoke. Everyone began to talk and laugh. A couple of guys got into an argument. George just sat there. Then one of them stood up and proposed a toast. Someone pulled out a bottle of vodka and went around pouring. There were several toasts. Then the leader called order and spoke. Another argument ensued. One of the men stormed out. The meeting lasted about 15 minutes. Then it ended. On the way out the translator said to George, "See. We can't run a meeting. We're working on it, though. It's better than two years ago. Everyone wanted to show you. What do you think?" "It's a lot like some of our meetings in the U.S.," George said, "only ours go on for hours." With that, the translator gave a howl and explained it to the other men, who became ecstatic. They gathered around George and pounded away at him. Then they let out a great cheer.

Not long after George's last visit, the Soviet Union dissolved. George is now retired. He still enjoys traveling, but, as far as I know, he has no plans to return to Russia. In 1998, Gorbachev surfaced as a guest speaker at the World Congress on Information Technology.

Journal Entry 72:

Sometime in the early '80s, my company held a symposium on the new programming language Ada. One executive after another rose to his feet and performed like Hitler in Munich in the '20s. I have never heard such oratory, except on television. It was like a tent meeting: Billy Sunday followed by Billy Graham. One by one, people came forward.

Programming was a "technology," like the steam engine or the transistor. I wondered how that could be. I learned the answer later. By declaration.

Ada, as it turned out, was not so much a programming language as a symptom, the first of many. Software would soon come to represent expertness and wealth. I had a professor in school who liked to say that if Aristotle were to reappear today he would marvel at what man has produced, but not at man himself. I think my professor was stretching a point. He was thinking of Aristotle the psychologist. Aristotle the logician would be astounded to learn that some of the richest people on Earth, only in their 20s and 30s, make their money practicing rude logic.

Within a short time, both the public and private sectors were coming down from the trees. Software companies were springing up like weeds in a dry summer. Consultants were handing out business cards identifying themselves as philosophers and metaphysicians. Publicists were making money off of pundits who were making money off of untried programming methods, and, for the first time in American history, everyone, both left and right, was in agreement: the faster we can write software, the better. (I shouldn't complain, though. I owe this house, my automobiles, my children's education, my pension, to the third epoch of software.)

And the government . . . the FAA wanted to get out in front. They bought Ada and all that came with it. The Advanced Automation System, the system to end all systems, the system that would overhaul air traffic control, was to be a Hollywood billboard for Ada and military standards and (somehow) programmer productivity. It didn't turn out that way.

9

. . .

SUPERVISION THROUGH LANGUAGE

The eloquence that diverts us to itself harms its
content.
  —MICHEL MONTAIGNE, *Essays, Education of Children*

It is not hard to pin down when the field of computer programming became the world of software, nor how and why it shifted from a fledgling, idiosyncratic practice, applied mostly to research and large computer systems, to a media phenomenon. It happened almost overnight, sometime in the 1980s. The technology had been in the works for years: microchips, network protocols, dense storage devices. It awaited the packaging and marketing, which emerged with the personal computer and the Internet. By 1990, computing on a large scale was readily available to the public. Since then, millions have become owners and users, if not programmers.

As computers became ubiquitous, great gobs of software followed, prompting both the private and public sectors to surge in opposing, yet complementary, directions. Greed, high expectations, hyperbole, and jargon were soon layered upon computer programming and programs, further obscuring a field already difficult to understand.

In the private sector, the rise of Microsoft was followed by the birth of thousands of software companies, all intent on duplicating the success of Bill Gates. (In the 1950s, in a similar vein, hundreds of manufacturing companies tried their hand at building computers; all but a handful fell by the wayside.) By 1990, software had become front-page news. We have been told that we are an information society. But the biggest splash has been made in the business section: "Software stimulates the economy; stock prices rise." "Computers and software are overhauling the workforce." Algorithms, once solely the province of mathematicians, were, and are, making millionaires of thousands of young men and women.

Software is now evident even in farm towns. For many of us, our first reckoning came with the automated teller machine. Then our favorite auto mechanic informed us that new cars were computerized. Then we waited for half an hour at the supermarket, while the computer controlling the registers got back online. Then came the Internet.

I wonder what Aristotle would think of all this. More than two thousand years ago, he wrote that even careful reasoning about one logical statement could lead to false conclusions. (Aristotle, I surmise, knew little, if anything, about the treacherous loop, the bread and butter of computer programs.) What would he think about millions of young men and women around the globe, daily compounding one logical expression upon another, loops and all, and sending the collective mass off to machines, to run at speeds measured in nanoseconds, and that the machines would control our finances, weapons, transportation and communications, energy, recreation, and education?

While cults were growing around commercial software, the U.S. government was nurturing one of its own. With one eye on the private sector and its apparent success, government agencies, not satisfied with or appreciating the herculean efforts to build the first national computer systems, began to devise even greater systems. To ensure that they could be built reliably and on time, the government mounted its own campaign on behalf of software. Tens of thousands of young men and women would *not* be allowed to render such complexity unattended. Thousands of pages of rules on how to develop computer systems were being developed by the Department of Defense, which, by virtue of its huge investment in technology and automation, led the drive for more regulation. A library of buzz-words was created. Legions of consultants were hired. And there would be a new programming language that could legislate pro-gramming: Ada.

Ada was named for Ada, the Countess of Lovelace, an obscure Englishwoman who was deemed to be the first programmer. She lived a hundred or so years before programmable computers were invented. The name Ada is catchy. It is rooted in history and thus suggests permanence. That was the hope when the U.S. Depart-ment of Defense created it in the 1980s: that Ada would forever stan-dardize the programming of computer systems.

Ada evolved from our experience with earlier procedural lan-guages. The consultants who helped fashion it were experts in PAS-CAL, PL/I, FORTRAN, ALGOL, COBOL, and even assembly languages. The objective was to build a language that would encour-age reliability while using the best features of its predecessors.

Ada shows the evidence of programming theory, such as struc-tured programming and programming types, and of design concepts for modules. The language encourages the formal specification of modules and their interfaces. It embeds features that simplify multi-programming and storage management and support input-output operations, lifting from the programmer some of the weight of deal-ing with the computer and its operating environment. Unfortu-nately, its richness makes training an issue. On the FAA's Advanced Automation System it took the average programmer four to six months to become proficient in Ada.

There was always much ado about Ada. Advocates became zealots. Critics abounded and were no less sharp. The loudest remark became famous within the field: "Ada is designed by committee." The rejoinder, somewhat oblique, was "Ada is more than just a programming language."

Ada quickly got tangled up with other issues: commercial practices, government standards, and the vaguely defined notions of software engineering and software productivity. Harry wrote to me asking if the Department of Defense's obsession with "software productivity" meant writing more code faster, or if it meant accelerating the "race to dependability," as he called it, by improving verification methods. I told him I thought it was the former.

By embedding methods in the language, like formally specified interfaces, and the use of types, Ada steers the programmer toward a standard that begins with the design of modules and carries through to debugging. But the title of this chapter derives not so much from the features of a language as from the standards for programming that the Department of Defense defined for it: a military standard called MIL-STD 2167. Adhered to on the FAA's Advanced Automation System, MIL-STD 2167 is the sum of every government move in opposition to contractor cost overruns and performance underruns since the building of the Bon Homme Richard.

The standard defines exactly how the contractors will carry out their work and document it. From the uncertain business of describing the system's requirements through the long-awaited and often-delayed installation of the system in the field, MIL-STD 2167 leaves no page unturned — literally. Virtually everything that can be known must be written down in the prescribed format: the system's anticipated behavior, the design, every program and test, every process, every penny spent and hour worked.

Take a single programming statement. We might want to know how many symbols it takes; how long it would take to write them; how it will be compiled or assembled; from what specification it was derived; how quickly or slowly it might run on a machine; what machine or machines it would run on; how much storage it would consume; whether it meets the standards of its syntax; how it would be tested, and the results; its relationship to the design; the risks of using that particular instruction; its relationship to the operating system under which it will execute; what databases it will reference, and how it will reference them; how the source text is converted to object form and how long that will take; the instruction's history, because it will surely change; its computational properties (Will it terminate, for example? What, if anything, will be done if an error is encountered?); how the possibility of writing it down incorrectly can be avoided through quality assurance procedures; how and to what degree it adheres to the "principles of software engineering." Most important, can it be reused to save time and effort? Certainly, we want to know how much it costs.

It turns out that writing a programming statement costs very little compared with writing about it. On large projects like the Advanced Automation System, there seems to be an inviolate ratio between the number of symbols in a computer program and the number composing its attendant literature, a sort of lexical pi.

Imagine a library of medicine, like that of the National Institutes of Health—only bigger. There, in shelves, both paper and electronic, is spelled out what is known about humans, from their DNA to their posturing at dinner parties, with entire floors dedicated to the cell, the organs, the various internal systems and their interconnections, everything up to and including the psychological and cultural (and a full wing earmarked for the collection and retention of data about the behavior of the people living in Los Angeles, California), all of this formulated relationally—with marked assistance from automation: the behavioral, the structural, the molecular, the immunological, and the historical compounded. It has taken centuries to accumulate and it is hardly used, because it is always out of date. This might give you some idea of the nature of MIL-STD 2167, Ada's praetorian guard.

Ironically, one of the early critics of Ada was C. A. R. Hoare, whose axiomatic approach to writing programs is grounded in the theory of types, of which Ada makes much. In his 1980 Alan Turing Award lecture, Hoare urged the U.S. government to use caution with Ada, and not to use the language in its then current state. He writes that "the price of reliability is the pursuit of the utmost simplicity. These objectives in Ada have been sacrificed in favor of power, supposedly achieved by a plethora of features and notational conventions, many of them unnecessary, and some of them, like exception handling, even dangerous." Hoare implored the United States not to use Ada to control airplanes and direct missiles.

In 1980, Hoare could not have known that far worse was in the offing than the way Ada supports recovery from errors. He could not have foreseen that the grassroots movement of software would erode the formal, mathematical approach to programming that he hoped would prevail, and that, in response to the software revolution, the U.S. government (as well as other governments) would add its own potion: strict supervision, resulting not in better software, nor a better process, but in mountains of documentation and more obfuscation. They crept in like ground fog: from the left, fast-food software, and from the right, government bureaucracy. The admixture created an atmosphere so noxious that it would cause many projects to commit suicide, including the FAA's Advanced Automation System.

In the early 1980s, I read a story in *Fortune* magazine about a new company called Rational. *Fortune* called their Rational R-1000 "an Ada machine." An Ada machine. Reading the words aloud, I thought they sounded decisive, like "the Turing machine." I wondered how it worked. The article speculated that this machine would transform programming.

The "Ada machine" *is* remarkable. Not long after reading the *Fortune* article, I was invited to see a demonstration of programmers using the Rational computer and its software. *Fortune* had overstated the case. The Rational R-1000 was not made of Ada; it is a computer like any other. But the designers had embedded several of the key compilation facilities in the computer's firmware. They built the operating procedures around Ada. The compiler even displays the correct syntax of each statement that fails the compilation, allowing the programmer to quickly correct the error.

The programmers at the demonstration were enthralled. One told me he thought he could write and compile a thousand Ada statements in a day. I knew then that, regardless of what the government meant by "software productivity," the programmers knew exactly what it meant.

Fortune was accurate in calling the Rational computer an Ada machine. It is an Ada machine, in the same sense that the great Red Sox hitter Ted Williams was a hitting machine. In 1955, I watched him take batting practice in Baltimore's Memorial Stadium. I was intoxicated with his effortless power. This must be how a programmer feels the first time he uses the Rational R-1000, and the second and the third. Turning out compilations at a phenomenal speed, the programmer wants to go on all night. If a manager were to ask that an inspection be held, he might get the same reaction I get when I interrupt my dog at his food dish.

Early in the Ada epoch, Rational was *the* specialist in the highly specialized world of Ada. The FAA decided to use Ada on the Advanced Automation System. At the time, IBM had few Ada products as effective as the Rational line, so about a dozen Rational computers were purchased and installed in IBM's development laboratory. Eventually, IBM's compilers and tools replaced the Rational configuration. But for a couple of years, software managers on the project found themselves in a situation not unlike that facing Charlemagne.

The king had a bent for seeing to things himself. He personally supervised the baptism of the Saxons, driving them into rivers sanctified upstream by his bishops. But there are limits. He ruled much of what is now Europe, and in the year 800 word traveled slowly, if it traveled at all. Charlemagne had great difficulty issuing capitularies, his edicts from the court at Aachen, to solidify the law of the land. Hardly anyone in the land could read. How to get the word out?

The story goes that Charlemagne knew the name of a man living near Aachan, a Frank who knew the name of everyone in Europe who could read. So, from time to time, the Emperor of the West would summon the man to court, arm him with one or two or several edicts, and send him to the provinces. Only through this narrow gate would the job get done. On the Advanced Automation System, the Rational R-1000 proved to be the gate. Without it, a failed project might have failed sooner.

Almost from the beginning, when it had become clear that there was money to be made in the margins of software, Ada the language was eclipsed by Ada the cottage industry. In time, Ada proved its worth on the Advanced Automation System project. Its chief asset turned out to be reliability, not coding speed. But the technical aspects of Ada are relatively unimportant to the story of software. The real woo-woo lies in the bandwagon. It's a good bet that far more money has been made in discussing Ada than in using it. Since 1980, a welter of Ada papers, conferences, texts of all kinds, curricula, digests, hotel rooms, flights, badges, slogans, and other paraphernalia has been circulating through the world economy.

The Advanced Automation System provided many opportunities to see the world on the taxpayer. A friend of mine, Mike, did Europe on Ada. Mike is a talented and sincere man. He not so much jumped on the bandwagon as he was swept onto it by IBM's management. Mike is from Tennessee. He likes to play the piano when he's not programming. He enjoys Cole Porter and show tunes. "Old things appeal to me," he says. He told me Vienna appealed to him. There was an Ada conference there, on the Danube, beneath the Carpathian foothills.

Mike wrote a paper on Ada and the conference committee accepted it. So one fine May afternoon he found himself strolling along the Ringstrasse with his camera slung over his shoulder mulling over what he would say about Ada's use of types. He told me that there was plenty to see: the Rathaus, the Burgtheater, and of course the Musikverein and the conservatory. This was, after all, the city of Mozart and Beethoven and Mahler, all of whom Mike said he would put right up there with Rodgers and Hammerstein.

When he got back he told me about the coffeehouses and the bierstube, where he drank mineral water and some beer. He told me about the fork breakfasts and the veal served with potatoes and a paprika sauce. He told me about Freud and how he thought the great man would now be an advocate of Prozac. He went to No. 19 Berggasse and saw the inner study of the Parterre office and the antiquities from Assyria and Egypt and the famous couch, which has come to grief with managed health care.

Next came Rome and the decisive role Ada's exception handler plays in preventing system failures—which it doesn't. But the paper was about the FAA's Advanced Automation System and air traffic control, so it was accepted. Mike took his wife to the Piazza Montecitorio and the Piazzale del Pincio. He showed me photos of a squadron of Ada aficionados in the Piazza Colonna, near the soiled column of Marcus Aurelius, who wrote, long before programming: "What a stranger he is who is surprised at anything which happens in life." In Rome, Mike says, the sole is good, but the waiters complained about his not drinking any wine. Somewhat chagrined, he told me of the scaffolding hung about the shoulders of many of the great buildings and statuary. But the vault of the Sistine Chapel impressed him. There he said he forgot about programming and the smell of the Tiber.

Mike turned out a number of papers and saw many other cities. I attended but one Ada conference, in Williamsburg. I had not written a paper, but I wanted to see what went on and it was only a couple of hours from my home. The conference was mostly unremarkable. But one night in the motel lobby, an ex-marine who published a magazine about Ada wrestled someone to the floor who had taken offense at his zeal. The magaziner wanted some generals court-martialed for "disobeying a direct order from the Pentagon." The generals had softened on Ada and not insisted that it be used on all projects. Of course, such cowardice in the face of the enemy could affect the popularity of Ada and thence this magaziner's income.

In the new epoch of software, things appear to change faster than programs run. No sooner had Ada become a government standard than it was mourned as passé. Ada is giving way to new languages (and cults) such as C and C++ and Java, which are more relaxed and trickier, and better suited to young programmers. Code can be turned out much faster in these languages than in Ada.

In December 1992, the Goddard Space Flight Center held a panel discussion to chew on the question "Is Ada Dying?" I did not attend, but I will offer an answer. Ada may be dying, but it will not die. Although there has been no great outpouring, thousands of Ada programs have indeed been compiled and executed. For this reason alone, Ada will endure. The relationship between a programming language and the symbols it produces is reciprocal. Each Ada program is a testament to the Ada compiler that gives it life, and vice versa. As long as there is an Ada program, there will be an Ada compiler and an Ada language. A programming language may fall out of favor, but it is unlikely to become extinct, nor will the programs written in it.

Journal Entry 75:

The faster programmers go, the more automated the task of programming, the more difficult management becomes. Even a good manager cannot stand between a programmer's keystrokes and the update of a file.

Washington Post advertisement—Wanted: C++ programmers who can think logically quickly, and managers of C++ programmers who can think on their feet and make split-second decisions.

I can imagine a day, not too far off, when programming is reduced to the selection of graphical icons. Young people, who will have been raised on video rather than texts, will prefer graphics, because taking in a picture requires less effort than reading and writing narratives. So they will build tools to suit their custom.

The president of Sun says that computers and software are fun. We just have to work on those who aren't into it. What could be more inviting than having a lot of fun and getting paid millions for it?

I thought of work as fun. It was fun because of the people I worked with, of any era. So I sound like a party pooper. Maybe it was those grueling years I spent in first-line management trying to hold programmers back, making them commit to schedules that included more design and inspection and testing than coding. Or maybe it's that I didn't make millions.

John Adams wrote that he studied war so that his sons could study history and philosophy, and their sons could study poetry. There may come a time when fathers and mothers study so that their children don't have to.

10

. . .

HOW TECHNOLOGY CHANGES METHODS

As soon as a discovery is made, a concrete applica-
tion is sought.
　　　　　　—Jacques Ellul, *The Technological Society*

Named for the building where John Cocke and his team designed it, the 801 was the first reduced instruction set computer, or RISC. A prototype of the 801 was built in 1974, the year the 9020 computer was first used in all domestic air traffic control centers. Unlike the 9020, the RISC was designed with programming in mind, especially programming with compilers. The RISC is three processors in one: an instruction-stream processor, a fixed-point processor for simple arithmetic, and a floating-point processor for high-precision scientific calculations and graphic applications. The processors run concurrently, but no programmer need know this.

IBM first used the RISC technology in its System/370 line of mainframes, the offspring of the System/360. For many years, IBM failed to pursue the use of the RISC in desktop computers. One of several opportunities IBM missed in the 1980s, the RISC chip did not show up in its workstations until 1984.

A workstation is not easy to distinguish from the personal computer you have in your house. The former is a powerful computer with an attached display and keyboard. The latter is a computerized display and keyboard. The difference has blurred. Both are very fast and both come with accoutrements now discussed in the cafeterias of what my grandmother called grammar school: a hard drive for storing data, a mouse for picking, a modem for communicating over the Internet.

A couple of years ago, Ed showed me his new workstation. He was about to run Taligent, a product sold by IBM, Apple, and Hewlett Packard. He powered on and the computer produced a farm, a beautiful scene, reminiscent of a Robert Altman movie. In the distance, behind rows of tulips, each of a slightly different color, there stood a near-perfect replica of a barn and silo, and an amiable farmhouse, like those found in Pennsylvania Dutch country, like the farm across from my office.

Before I could take it all in, we were telemarketing. There were windows upon windows. One contained icons for folders, stationery, and documents, even trash. There was a window for business cards and one for financial spreadsheets. Another invited me to select one of eight natural languages by dragging and dropping the mouse on the appropriate flag. At the bottom of the screen, a ticker rolled off the daily stock quotes. I browsed through a catalog selling gloves, soft garden gloves, goat skin, and suede, the textures rendered as if snipped from "Gardener's Eden." The phone book was the most impressive. I picked a client's number from a list. The phone dialed automatically. Had voice activation been installed, I could have simply spoken the number. All the while, clips of the movie *Dracula* were being shown in the upper left part of the screen. Movies, not stills. The protagonist was sucking the blood out of some innocent, while I contemplated my next sales call.

As I left Ed's house, I thought about the powerful as miniature. As a child, I believed that power emanated from large things — large people, large machines, and large buildings. My father took me to Wall Street when I was about five. He told me that powerful people ran the country from those big buildings.

My guess is that a new kind of myth will arise, if it hasn't already: the technological myth. Mythology as handed down over the centuries may slowly evaporate. Cyrene, the water nymph, the mother of Aristaeus, the beekeeper, will drown (again) and her place in the hearts and minds of children will be taken by other depictions, rendered in splendid graphics on 21-inch displays. Today's children already thrill to technology. They are firmly in the grasp of the artificial as surely as Achilles was in the grasp of Apollo.

Harry once commented: "It's a good thing there is more government supervision of programming now. Programming is harder than ever to see." In the era of punched cards, there was a machine or a tool for each job. You could tell who was doing what. Programmers coded on paper designed for keypunching. Flow charting templates helped with logic design. Sometimes typewriters were used for high-level design. The physical brought regimentation and authority. Lines were well marked. Only those people called programmers working under the flag of programming wrote code; not everyone.

A friend who worked on NASA's Space Shuttle System tells of the lab manager where flight control software was tested. Julius, an older fellow, was always there, it seemed, logging in the card decks, explaining the rules and regulations about entering the lab to novice programmers. Everyone learned and obeyed.

I had a similar job my first year at NAFEC, but without the authority. I was a go-between for the programmers and the FAA operators. I logged patches to the software — corrections in the form of punched cards that would overlay computer storage — before each test run. There was continual controversy. Should I be allowed to insert the cards in the card feeder, and punch "enter" and "end-of-file"? Or was my job limited to logging the patches and handing them over to the operator? This was never resolved satisfactorily. I learned much later that when it comes to job security, no job is too small.

By the mid-1970s, programmers on most large systems were using video display terminals, or VDTs. These looked much like today's personal computers, but they contained no software. They were attached to a mainframe computer, almost like a video keypunch machine. The programming languages had not changed much. We wrote our programs in assembly language, FORTRAN, COBOL, PL/I. But the keyboard and display replaced coding sheets. The terminal gave birth to the death of erasure: no more scraping away mistakes—you simply backspaced and typed. Where once humans intervened, entire databases could be summoned with a few keystrokes. I was glad my father made me take typing in high school (just in case I went to work for an insurance company).

With terminals, coding was easier. They also had an impact on design. By the mid-1970s, designing programs was catching on, slowly. Flow charts were replaced with design languages. The nonintelligent terminals limited the design notation. VDTs were not built for drawing, so most designs were described lexically. Some projects used a syntax similar to that of a high-level programming language (IBM developed an Ada Process Design Language, for example). Some projects used a syntax that, when "compiled," resulted in printed diagrams, such as data flow diagrams.

Terminals encouraged shortcuts. Programmers went too fast, largely because copying was faster. Source libraries resided on the mainframes and were universally available. It was all too easy to copy someone's program, to use as a template, and then forget to make one or two of the changes in the process of tailoring it to your specification. Fearing the worst, Harlan Mills, at the time an IBM Fellow and adviser to the division president, warned against terminals: "Hurried programs will bristle with errors." Mills was fond of saying that programmers write programs without having read any, including their own. He preferred punched cards.

Terminals brought social changes. At first, too few terminals were available to put one on each desk. So the project allotment was put in terminal rooms: two terminals to a table. There was space for a listing next to the terminal. If you needed a document as well, you held it on your lap. By midmorning the terminal rooms were full.

The terminal rooms improved communications. There were distractions, of course, but cooperation between programmers, and their programs, increased. If someone had just finished debugging a macro, he or she would announce the name of the library. You could fetch it and look at it right then. Programmers discussed their programs and bugs and computer time, the latest standard, some new operating system discovery, a restriction on the size of arrays, the awful severity of the new configuration control package.

Inspections came in as punched cards left. An inspection is a method by which programmers read and critique, in a kind way, another's program or design or test cases. My first impression of inspections was negative. They slowed me down. My colleagues and I had acclimated to terminals and the quick turnaround they offered. Looking back, inspections displaced the time and effort we once put in desk-checking our work when it had to be keypunched, when a mistake could cost hours or days. In the beginning, no one knew the cost of inspecting; it was not built into the schedules. So we had to work more overtime than usual. Most of us would have preferred to avoid inspections. On several counts, they were painful.

Inspections are an important step in moving programming toward engineering. Civil engineers have inspected each other's work for centuries. Public works deserve scrutiny and deliberation. So much depends on their soundness. Of greater importance, perhaps, is the impact that inspections have on management. Inspections make visible the invisible. And they are communal—they bring programmers and their programs together by plan. But their greatest asset is more subtle: inspections create milestones. Completing the design or the coding of a module can be measured not through a status report but through a commitment that binds the quality of the product to the time and cost to produce it.

Inspections are conducted by peers. Managers do not attend, although they see the results. This is a crucial adaptation of the Heisenberg Uncertainty Principle, wherein observing the experiment can change it. If managers are watching, the true number of errors may not be revealed. It has been suggested that the public discovery and tallying of errors, even among peers, is enough to discourage making them.

Over the years, inspections have become more formal. Invitations are issued. About three days in advance, prospective participants are told the time and place of the inspection meeting and given the material to be inspected. The amount of material should be modest, in the interest of intellectual control. The meeting is presided over by a moderator, who has graduated from indoctrination sessions to prepare for the role. A presenter, a sort of ad hoc deacon who cannot be the author of the material, reads aloud from the exhibit, but not line by line. The meeting lasts about two hours.

The errors and questions are scrupulously recorded by the moderator. Participants keep track of the amount of time they spent preparing for the meeting, reading and inspecting the exhibit, and documenting their findings. A separate organization, quality assurance, often placed strategically within the company or the project, approves the procedures for conducting inspections, monitors their conduct, and collects statistics. The statistics help determine the cost of finding and fixing errors early in the programming life cycle.

I write about this as if it were the norm. But after 40 years of industrial programming, many organizations do not perform inspections.

Harry believed that as software development became more automated, programmers would be less careful and exacting. Exercising the principles of engineering would lose favor. Clinton, who worked on several large projects with me, including air traffic control, says that what we were doing was really engineering, and it happened to involve programming. He has worked for America Online for about four years now and adds that "at AOL there is no engineering; it's just programming."

Today, in software development laboratories around the world, there are workstations and a mountain of programs to go with them, not quite like Taligent's telemarketing offering, but similar. Marketing representatives call these programs tools, or technologies. But they are just computer programs. Like compilers, they are used to write other programs, for nuclear power plants, strategic weapons systems, and hospitals. They are a by-product of our desire to automate software development. Edsger Dijkstra, who mixes his own ink, told Patricia on the bluffs of Salve Regina that tools are wonderful for managing complexity: "So good, in fact, they encourage it."

Sometimes these tools are advertised under the title of computer-aided software engineering, or CASE. CASE tools roll together the typewriter, the plastic template, the keypunch, and sometimes the thinking. On the Advanced Automation System project, as I walked down the hall, I could not tell whether programmers were working out their ideas incrementally with precise abstractions or just coding.

The project, heavily into everything automated, tried compilable designs. The programmers wrote millions of lines of Ada "design." The idea was to shorten the coding cycle. But the result was no design. The programmers, quite naturally, slid into the details. The experiment, highly touted by IBM management, failed. When the time for design reviews arrived, the software design was conveyed using transparencies, developed just for the occasion.

Some projects have found benevolent products that encourage uniformity without penalizing initiative. When there are hundreds of programmers, and all but a few want to do things their own way, tools, used properly, keep the work lined up and heading in the same general direction. Everyone records design or test cases or schedules the same way, and the artifacts are captured electronically so they can be updated more easily.

The latest tools run on workstations, which, unlike the VDTs, support drawing and graphics. Graphics tend to encourage abstraction, which has a positive effect on the design process. Using graphical tools, combined with text, programmers may be more inclined to think conceptually *and* precisely, and avoid plunging into the details before they have grasped the big picture. But graphics can also deceive. Unlike mathematical notation, pictures can give the *appearance* of symmetry and coherence and completeness and avoid the real matter.

Workstations have moved programmers back into the safety of offices, where we started. The programming cycle is now largely electronic, although we generate more paper than ever and need more printers and couriers. Programmers still get together for inspections, but electronic mail has replaced the rap of terminal rooms, which are gone, although some companies use bullpens, like those at NAFEC.

On the Advanced Automation System project, we were preoccupied with getting together. We met many times a day in large, comfortable conference rooms. The scheduling of meetings and conference room assignments was automated. Automation bears its own standard. Meeting became easier, so we did more of it. Dozens of groups, at every level of every organization, met almost daily on one subject or another. Many subjects overlapped. So many people met all day.

At NAFEC, in the 1960s, there were no meeting rooms and, as a result, very few meetings. When I think about those early years, I cannot recall attending more than a few meetings. We worked well together, between departments, with the FAA, with other contractors. Did we avoid meetings simply because there were few places to meet? My department got together occasionally, but we met in our manager's office. There was room to bring in a chair or two. Mostly we stood, which helped move the meeting along. On the 9020 System project, we seemed to know what we were about and wanted to get to it. On the Advanced Automation System, we were never quite sure. So we discussed everything at length. Despite all the automation, we eventually talked ourselves out of work.

ARE THERE ABSOLUTE LIMITS ON THE SIZE OF SOFTWARE?

Journal Entry 76:

I've always been fascinated by size. Nature does not truck with scale, at least in the biological sphere. There is a good reason why elephants cannot fly. But what about man's productions? We have built enormous buildings that will not collapse in the fiercest wind. We can launch into space and assemble a space station the size of a shopping center. In the digital age, what does size mean? Can a million modules be built to operate correctly as if they were one?

The answer depends on how you define "one." If you think of a single project, there are certainly limits. Trying to write and test a billion lines of software under one contract seems absurd. But, considering the evolution of software over many projects, we have not yet reached a practical limit.

As new generations of computers and their operating systems emerge, their antecedents are absorbed. In the language of computing, the vestigial functions are emulated. This is one reason why operating systems require more and more storage to operate. In 1999, if we could see it, the inside of a computer would look like a Chinese box, one digital box hidden within another. The programs written for the PC operating system DOS reside within the Windows 95 operating system. The first versions of DOS were written by IBM, so it is not unlikely that entire procedures of DOS were copied from OS/360, which was written in the early 1960s.

We can look at size from another vantage point: interfaces. Systems interfacing with other systems. Whatever you may call it, connectivity, integration, or open communications, there is no denying that digital systems grow not just by absorption but by annexation. This is man-made evolution at its best—or worst, depending on your moral bent. It is no exaggeration to claim that a good part of the planet is already "wired." In no small measure, this is what is driving the American stock market.

But the problem of limits remains for single projects, where absorption and annexation are small factors. Recently, the IRS, having failed to pull off a multibillion-dollar overhaul of its computer systems in one chunk, signed a contract of equal size with Computer Sciences Corporation to try it again. Obviously, the IRS, unlike nature, is not respectful of mass, in this case, intellectual mass.

11

. . .

SIZE AND INTELLECTUAL GRAVITY

The chapter house at Batalha—one of the widest
stone vaults in medieval architecture—collapsed
twice during construction and was finally built by
prisoners condemned to death.
    —STEPHEN JAY GOULD, *Ever Since Darwin*

If programming symbols were made of steel, we would surely notice men and women straining to hoist thousand-pound beams with a single hand. But alas, their weight is intellectual, so we turn away.

The steady advance of technology, the steady advance of the small, the invisible, or the nakedly invisible—for layers of technology have extended our perceptions while blunting them—has enlarged systems and our expectations for them. The smaller the machine, it seems, the larger the concepts. The complexity of practice has always dwarfed the simplicity of theory. But where can we draw the line in software?

How many generations of programmers can fit inside a single loop? How far can recursion be stretched before it snaps? How much

111

light can pass between the truth and falsity of a proposition? Can we even know what is mathematical and what is biological? Does the system retain more mathematical states within a sequence of its operations than it can recover before a user gives up? And what of his neighbors? Who will hear the crack of brick and wallboard as water tries desperately to find its level on the digital plain? Can marched legions, working like slaves, led by a marble tyrant, make it up in the end? How much lift can we expect from a giant, whose volume grows an exponent faster than its surface area?

E. F. Shumacher, in *Small Is Beautiful*, suggests that a city of more than 500,000 is not habitable. In such a place, dissimilar economies circle around one another like proteins, breeding unrest. Schools decay. Life is tedious and risky. Waste abounds. Citizens edge toward social poles, then take refuge in the status quo.

The effects of a gargantuan computer system are less well known and as hard to abridge. Such systems are rare, but not because of gravity and the great medieval forces but because of the loss of intellectual control. Can a few designers design a system that can be built by a few hundred that can be used productively by a few million?

Thousands of papers and hundreds of books have been written about developing and verifying the correctness of an algorithm, a programming procedure. Even within a procedure, fascinating problems exist—for example, verifying the correctness of a loop, one of the most complex structures in logic. We should not abdicate our investigations at this level. We know that a single instruction caused the Ariane-5 rocket to blow up, and that the specification of a single variable containing a date may cause untold problems and cost billions of dollars to find and fix as we approach the year 2000. But, in practice, writing and testing a 50-line procedure is manageable. Unmanageable, or nearly unmanageable, is writing and testing 100,000 such procedures, with interfaces in the thousands, all of which must be integrated and tested as a single system on a single project with organizations working in parallel.

All systems change as they are being developed. That we get as far as we do on large projects is a miracle. The whole thing is implausible. On the Advanced Automation System project, tracking the developing system, its documentation, and the various versions running in the various laboratories, and keeping it all synchronized, proved to be an almost insurmountable problem. Change is constant. Imagine building the Brooklyn Bridge, starting from both sides of the East River with two teams, each changing the requirements specifications and the design as they go, both praying the two meet in the middle.

In software development, from the first day after the first day and forever after, at least two versions of the system exist, sometimes three or four. Many dimensions must be kept straight, from the specifications to the test cases. First there is "This program shall compute this number." Then, later, "that number." Then, in source code, "IF (this) AND (that) THEN . . . ABORT." Then, in the computer, "00000101010111111." Later this is verified, with the help of more narrative and more code: "PRINT 'ABORT' => (more ones and zeroes)."

On large projects, these various forms are rendered by different organizations, barely acquainted with one another. One specifies. Another codes. A third tests. And each writes thousands of pages, documenting each task.

The dependencies are spidery. Team A specifies programs for team B, while B codes programs previously specified by A, just as team C is testing programs previously coded by B. Team C finds a problem in one of B's programs. Team B interrupts its coding on the next version to fix the program C is testing. This is because A's prose was obscure or indifferent. Then there is D, the programs used to automate the specifying, coding, and testing. To keep all of this straight there is a fifth column, E: it connects A, B, C, and D, showing how one is related to another, a spectacular form of knotty invariance, beads that wander across and through the specifications, code, and tests, indicating that this statement in this program can be traced to that program, which calls another, which is a refinement of this design statement, which can be said to be fathered by that requirement, which will be tested by this test. Think of capturing the relationship between the esophagus, stomach, and liver during a leisurely Italian meal. The relationships are liquid, more like wine than gnocchi.

Then, at four in the afternoon, a specification is changed that deletes a program being feverishly tested in the laboratory. And so distorted relationships are frozen in time, while invariant relationships fall out of date. E is never correct.

Defining the size of software has always been somewhat seat-of-the-pants. No method lacks pitfalls. Moving from the inside out, the purest and least informative approach is to measure the number of potential mathematical states a software product or system might attain. The number of possible program paths in the 9020 System was once estimated to be 10 to the power of 11,801. I don't know who did the analysis or how they arrived at such a number, but it doesn't matter much. All we can learn from this figure is that any software system, regardless of its size and complexity, is mathematically enormous. Imagine the local power company measuring each dwelling's consumption of electricity in terms of electrons, or maybe quarks.

The 9020 System was also measured in terms of source lines of code, or programming statements. In 1970 the number was 500,000. It represents code written in assembly language and in JOVIAL, a high-order language, each statement of which, when compiled, generates in the range of two to twenty assembly language statements. The 500,000 mixes the raw assembly language and the JOVIAL. The number of assembly language instructions generated by each JOVIAL statement does not figure into the calculation. The count is an admixture. The 500,000 includes the logical statements and the variables. It does not include commentary. It does not include the software written to run diagnostics, build the system, and support its testing. But the number is pure in one sense: it represents the amount of code *custom-developed* for the 9020. No software was copied from other projects, and no commercial software companies existed from which to draw algorithms. On the other hand, the 500,000 lines of code were written at least three times.

Some projects have attacked the size problem by counting the number of modules and applying bounds to the number of source lines of code per module. But what constitutes a module?

Another approach to size assays the number of functions, or features, the software will enact. There is considerably more variability here. The line of code approach at least deals with the source material, the symbols. Counting functions—the popular term is *function points*—can be more misleading than counting lines of code. Functions are not mathematically precise abstractions of the software; they are generalities. One program calculates a square root; another generates a report. What have we learned about the cost of the programming effort, about the probability of a failure, about the consequences of a failure? Counting functions places us in the zone of concrete generalities.

Size matters. I wish we could calculate software size accurately and in a standard way. We can't. Software is too fluid, its nature too organic. It defies virtually every model we would impose on it. Its elusive manner will prevail. But its elusiveness has made and will continue to make millions for its methodologists as surely as the conveniences it produces have made and will continue to make billions for its makers. Software, at the core, on the periphery, in the penumbra, in its every aspect, is a trove.

I have leaned heavily on lines of code to measure software size, elusive or not. It is, I am afraid, a third of a loaf. But it is the least dissembling third. For the sake of argument, I will use it now.

President Reagan, inspired by Buck Rogers, whom he had admired since childhood, asked the United States to build a huge system—SDI, the Strategic Defense Initiative—to thwart Soviet missiles in outer space. SDI would involve software (something Buck Rogers knew nothing about), much of it located in outer space. Estimates put the size of the developed software near a hundred million programming statements.

When computers like the 9020 took up an entire building and processed only 3 megabytes of data, a software package the size of 100 million lines of code was unthinkable. It is now thinkable. Setting aside whether we can write and integrate 100 million lines of code, so that it operates dependably, the executable images of such a suite would fit in computers small enough to launch into space. On the surface, there is nothing to stop us.

About twelve years after the start of the Advanced Automation System, and two years before its termination, the software development cycle began to groove. The mapping of programmers to modules was optimal. The laboratories and the system configuration were tightly controlled. The programmers were proficient in Ada. Hundreds of tools had been developed. Testing and debugging, from the unit to the system level, were thorough and efficient. Management sparkled; the earned value system was practiced fanatically, leaving no doubt where we were, where we had been, and where we were going. It was my good fortune to be involved in the analysis and supervision of the software during this time. I collected and studied as much data as was available, in part because it was my job and in part because I was curious. I learned that, after many false starts, changes in management, frequently renovated methods and procedures, years of churning requirements, and dozens of setbacks, an organization—amazingly committed after experiencing so much defeat—could operate smoothly and in a way that was satisfying to most, if not all, of its staff.

I learned that the nearly 500,000 source lines of very complicated code, which supported the highly distributed system that was to become the first major phase of the Advanced Automation System—the Initial Sector Suite System—had been written at least three times, not unlike the original 9020 System. I learned that, in the final two years, the software organization found by inspection an average of 11 potential faults per module; that at the system level, an average of 300 valid system failures were discovered, fixed, and retested in a month, although the number could exceed 400 at times; that the average size of a fix ran to over 30 lines of Ada and crossed modules; and that fewer than 4 percent of the fixes did not work and failed verification.

I learned that, in the final two years, the organization—including programmers, systems engineers, configuration control specialists, testers, lab engineers, the entire array of managers, planners, technical leaders, cost engineers, financial staff, executives, logistics experts, contracts personnel, quality assurance, project support staff, and secretaries—could produce 100,000 source lines of working, real-time, mission critical, safety-rated software in a year. The code was not copied, purchased, or stolen; it was developed in our labs. Over 70 percent of the technical budget was spent on verification activities such as inspections and testing; only 30 percent was spent designing and writing code.

Estimating the work on a linear basis, and assuming the same emphasis is placed on verifying the software, developing the 100 million lines of SDI software would take a thousand years. Of course, the effect of increasing software size is not linear, it is exponential. (Here we must take the mathematical view; for the system to operate dependably, the number of states is the decisive issue.) So maybe we should allocate a gang of millennia for the job. Completing the SDI software may well occupy 99.99999 percent of man's entire time on Earth—and then some.

This would be the case only if the SDI organizations were to spend 70 percent of their money verifying the software. But nothing would prevent them from writing 20 million lines of code a year— say, twenty companies working in parallel, each writing a million lines a year—and spending 2 percent of the budget inspecting and testing. Then the software development could be done in five years and finish well before nuclear weapons become obsolete.

Harry writes: "Corporate and government executives, committed to building such systems, are dumbfounded. They cannot appreciate that the digital space, air traffic, communications, and weapons systems are as unique as the Brooklyn Bridge, once-in-a-generation feats of engineering. They stand, unawed, as the construction of some invisible Cheops proceeds, forward, then backward, then forward again, with its tonnage and its intricate network of tombs and sarcophagi, embedded within massive forms, scrupulously engineered and placed in perfect alignment, supported by logistical systems as complex as the tomb itself—which, when completed, keeps in harmony the land, machines, society, the state, and its economy. Once in a while, they get out-of-context reports about a single task in progress, such as the digging of a trench, and wonder, What could be the problem?"

THIS IS NOT ROCKET SCIENCE!

Article in the *Washington Post*:

COMPUTER PROBLEMS TAXING IRS

The Treasury Department yesterday acknowledged that its decade-long, multibillion dollar effort to modernize the Internal Revenue Service's computers is "badly off the track" and must be rethought from top to bottom.

The project has been "more grand and more elaborate than was consistent with feasible budgetary reality," says Deputy Treasury Secretary Lawrence Summers. "Nevertheless, some taxpayers can file from home computers," says IRS Commissioner Margaret Milner Richardson.

The problem "is not technology" claims subcommittee Chairman Jim Lightfoot (R-Iowa). "They're probably out there building the roof right now [but] nobody's dug the foundation anywhere yet. The plumbing's probably going to end up in the living room and while you flush the commodes the lights come on in the garage. This is a $4 billion fiasco."

The Tax Systems Modernization effort is the second giant government computer program to consume years of work and billions of dollars without producing the promised payoff. The FAA's Advanced Automation System cost the nation . . .

Lightfoot: "This is not rocket science!"

Mr. Lightfoot is correct, of course. Rockets have a long history. The Chinese used them for fireworks in the eleventh century. They operate on the principle that if a small part of the rocket's total mass is ejected at high speed, the remaining mass will be impelled forward in the opposite direction. Incrementally, the rocket gets a bigger and bigger boost as more propellant mass is ejected. Eventually, when the residual rocket mass is minuscule, the boost becomes enormous. The integrated effort of these nonlinear boosts can be calculated as a simple logarithm using the variables of speed and mass, both of which are discussed at length in high schools by science teachers and football coaches.

Rocketry is not quite that simple. As work goes, it's complicated, more complicated than a doorknob or a pulley. Things can go wrong with rockets and often do. But we've put some time in on rocketry—codified a lot of it, in fact—and, except for the occasional backyard amateur, it is practiced by scientists. Programming is practiced by anyone with a computer, its history is largely anecdotal, and, at its roots, it is so complicated that we'd prefer not to ask.

The IRS project was like the FAA's Advanced Automation System project. Neither used rockets. Both agencies believed that the new generation of computers, small enough to give to every user—thus distributing the system and increasing its complexity—and powerful enough to support new and more sophisticated software, would solve their problems in one fell swoop. *Large was beautiful.* Imagine a rocket the size of New York City, which, if you looked at it from the ionosphere, might appear small. Over there is Harlem, and there is the Village, and down there, under the cables, Staten Island. Look a bit closer: there is the room near Washington Square where Joseph Brodsky wrote his poems in exile. Can you make out the edge of the letter "W" where he wrote "Water is glass's most public form / Man is more frightening than his skeleton?"

SOFTWARE AD SELLS FOR $1M A MINUTE DURING SUPER BOWL
YEAR 2000 PROBLEM GENERATES BILLIONS IN
PRIVATE SECTOR REVENUE

Journal Entry 81:

Religion holds sway because of its closely guarded secrets. Interpreters called priests are needed. Software has become a religion of sorts. Its priests are the presidents of various technology companies and consultants in the public sector. Their job is to sell. It helps that the field is sprayed with buzzwords.

I once promised a customer that my company could write one million lines of software in a year and a half. When asked how we could do that, I said we'd write about 200,000 lines and re-use it five times. I knew better. If I had been in the business of designing an office building, I might be writing this from prison.

The computer scientists and mathematicians I read in the '60s are either dead or quiet, their energy displaced by the tumult around us: thousands of software companies, the wealth of Gates, the technology stocks, *Wired* magazine. It's easy to get loss in the fuss. Today's heroes are not mathematicians or engineers; they are young CEOs and even younger digital second-story men who can break into an information warehouse without leaving a trace.

I don't hold much hope for software as an engineering discipline. Not that it can't be, but we don't want it badly enough. I know. I sold out. I've ridden more bandwagons than I can count. We've all learned that there is money to be made in this field.

On the Advanced Automation System, the FAA wanted the latest in everything and IBM gave it to them, especially re-usable software. Unhappily, it was the programmers that were re-used. The software? It wasn't re-used as much as it was rewritten—many times over.

12

. . .

THE MARKETING OF SCIENCE

*We've had the goddam Age of Faith, we've had the
goddam Age of Reason. This is the Age of Publicity.*
— WILLIAM GADDIS, *The Recognitions*

Every field has its ups and downs. Most of them can be charted, with
some accuracy, in terms of sales. Here is a story in which sales, mathematics, and religion converge.

About twenty-five hundred years ago, Pythagoras and his fol-
lowers married two profound concepts: the transmigration of souls
and number theory. They believed that numbers are sacred, that
they concentrate meaning. In the interest of purification they followed strict moral, ascetic, and dietary rules. They held animals in
high esteem and protected rather than slaughtered them. They were
popular among women because they preached equality between
the sexes.

When it came to numbers, the Pythagoreans were rationalists.
Irrational numbers—numbers that cannot be expressed by an ordinary fraction—were heretical. One day someone discovered that,

using the Pythagorean theorem, you could not prove the existence of an isosceles triangle with sides of length one using only rational numbers. In carrying out the proof, the square root of two shows up. The square root of two is an irrational number.

The story goes that a few of the sect were charged with guarding the secret of irrational numbers and that one was assassinated for threatening to divulge the information. As time went on, the Pythagoreans expanded their religious practices. When their mathematical premises foundered, they turned more to marketing their beliefs, until, as often happens, their zeal became too annoying. They were then run out of town.

Lewis Thomas, writing about medicine in his father's day, shortly after the turn of the century, describes one of the latest theories. It was felt that disease in general could be attributed to "the absorption of toxins from the lower intestinal tract." For over a decade, cathartics and variations of the enema became the treatment of choice for just about everything.

Today, diet is considered a critical factor in heart disease. We don't know why coronary vessels deteriorate. So we stock bookstores with paperbacks that attribute disease to lifestyle. Some offer great recipes. In a similar vein, if you browse through a software journal or magazine, you'll notice advertisements for methods. Some of them may reveal the outcroppings of a deep truth, to be discovered many years later, repudiated, and then, after review by committee, made orthodox. Some may be nonsense. Either way, when methods coil around marketing, it's hard to distinguish business from engineering and science.

In the world of software, business is winning. Testifying before Congress, Bill Gates declared: "I'm just a software engineer." My guess is that Mr. Gates has not studied the effects of programming faults on system failures, nor asked his second-line managers to sign off on module test plans and reviewed the results, nor does he worry about the consistency of error messages. Thousands of programmers who practice engineering would take offense at Gates's statement.

But they are seeing the world upside down. Gates *is* a software engineer. Today a software engineer is someone who owns thousands of shares in, sells, makes speeches about, and manipulates the market of the offerings we call software. (Gates has gone well beyond the ordinary, even among software engineers. He sits on the board of Icos, a biotechnology company, whose chief product is aimed at supplanting the impotence drug Viagra.)

Visit America Online. There you will see programmers logged on to their work and the minute-by-minute stock reports. Nearly every employee has a piece of the company. Clinton says that when AOL's stock is going up, productivity increases; when it goes down, morale suffers, and productivity goes down. Selling automation will soon become automated, effortless, like child's play. Just the other day, I heard a young girl, about 12, tell her friend on the phone: "It's all set up. Yeah . . . It's got Windows 95." Marketing without blood; Mao's way: kids first. And soon the air force, country X, will fall in behind Jennie.

Part of a letter by Harry from Morocco: "The race to aggrandizement attended by—no, driven by—expectations has added and blurred layers of abstraction. Imagine a pyramid, the northeast face. Let me call it the pyramid of abstractions. At the bottom, on the left, a section is outlined in blue, behind which lie the secrets of engineering and science. At the bottom, on the right, a section is outlined in red, the color used by the Holy Roman Church to commemorate the feasts of the martyrs. Herein lie the secrets of marketing. Think your way up the pyramid face, where the colors merge, where shades of meaning impose themselves and distinctions begin to disappear. Near the top lie vaults, ancient in origin, that blend science, engineering, advertising, the edicts of kings, and bits of theology. In this zone the vestiges of alchemy cling. Here you take your chances. Here, behind the dissembling stone, it's likely your comprehension of an idea will not match mine or Wyatt's or Ned's, who only a few years ago worried about his money, but now frets over the effect the Year 2000 problem will have on his son's medical condition."

As we approach the next millennium, software salesmen-engineers are having a field day. Taking advantage of a vocabulary that changes monthly, obscuring some of the most difficult mathematical concepts ever conceived, the software salesmen-engineers are enticing ordinary folks to buy what they cannot fathom.

A couple of years ago, a press release was issued by Miller Freeman, Inc., in *Wall Street and Technology:*

> . . . [R]oughly 450 Wall Street systems developers packed an auditorium at Metropolitan Life to learn the ins and outs of object-oriented (OO) programming. Organizers had to change locations twice to accommodate the overwhelming response from financial houses either implementing or investigating this technology. OO is taking New York by storm. That's because OO eases the process of dealing with rapidly evolving financial instruments. "Some of the most creative uses of object oriented technology are on the trading floor," says Susan Cohen, a senior analyst at Forrester Research in Cambridge, Mass. OO is revolutionizing the role traders play in the design of new products and in the tracking of product life cycles. Instead of waiting for programmers to design financial products, some traders can assemble new hedging strategies by simply pointing to objects. Once the technology has truly taken hold, experts see the chance for the integration between the front and back office functions.

The term *object* has become the most titillating word in the brief history of software. It has outstripped *structured*, which held the lead for years. Like *structured*, the word *object* has been worked over pretty well by a raft of fields, including mathematics, philosophy, psychology, the arts, biology, and a few more. The word is so conceptual that it's easy for everyone at the dinner table to nod his or her head and say, "Yes, I know what you mean," and each comprehend something different.

Here is a quote from Uta Hagen's *Respect for Acting*:

> To act is to do, not to think. The actor's thinking depends on
> the subjective process of weighing the course of action by a
> contrast of inner and outer objects. The fight against intru-
> sions on true thought can be conquered only by strengthening
> and enlarging the circle of inner objects. But it must be clear
> to you now that if any inner object in the play is not real to
> you, it will have no consequence in producing genuine
> thought.

Are these objects in any way related to the objects in programming?

They are. Programs are mental work, mental models of the
real world. "Much of the heterogeneity and complexity of current
theory is clarified by an approach that takes as its starting point the
dialectical tension between these competing strategies for understanding object relations, one preserving the original drive model
and the other replacing it with a fundamentally different model, one
more object-oriented." This was not copied from the latest software
journal. It is an excerpt from *Object Relations in Psychoanalytic
Theory*, Jay Greenberg.

Everyone worries about objects, it seems. The logician Willard
Van Orman Quine wrote an entire book about objects, called *Word
and Object*. You can read all 300 pages of it. Or you can read
Quine's summary in his invocation to the muse: "Ontology recapitu-
lates philology."

If software objects are now integral to our nation's economy,
they must be something to worry about. My neighbor, now retired,
has been working on his personal computer for about two years. He
gets the magazines, he says. Not too long ago he asked me if I am
object oriented.

Behind the scenes and the brochures, software experts argue
about the arcane. The most complex enterprise on Earth can no
longer do with just logic and variables. As the field becomes more

obscured, debate follows, as it did in the fourth century. Arius, who could not quite fathom Christ as both wholly man and wholly God, went east with the notion of Christ as demigod, thus creating Arianism. It was later condemned, found to be similar to Sabellianism, which also favored what became known as consubstantialism. The First Council of Nicaea was convoked and a tide of nuances surfaced. Splinter groups formed, debating terms for centuries, as Arianism and its offshoots took root with the Goths and Visigoths, who later swept the credo back through Europe.

The objects referred to in the article in *Wall Street and Technology* are *not* the same as the objects used in object-oriented programming. (They are related perhaps. As Harry once quipped, "Everything in programming is someone's relation.") The article alludes to the use of icons that appear on workstation displays. The icons, or objects, represent words; for example, a picture of a filing cabinet represents the term *filing cabinet*.

In object-oriented programming, the term *object* means something much more complicated. Objects in programming take their cue from mathematics. Mathematicians define relations (equations, formulas) in terms of a signature. The signature has three parts: operators, objects, and a set of distinguishing elements within the set of objects. In mathematics, objects by themselves have no meaning. This is also true in object-oriented programming. An example of a set of objects is the set of positive integers. Without operators applied to the set, there can be no structure and thus no meaning. (As with programming, mathematics has become far more complex over time. Today's math students puzzle over group theory and category theory. If you are interested in the application of category theory to computer programming, I recommend reading *Algebraic Approaches to Program Semantics*, by Michael A. Arbib and Ernest G. Manes.)

In object-oriented programming, programmers can define modules in terms of a class of objects and the procedures that give the objects structure. A class of objects may be the set of automobiles, or it may be the set of Volvos, depending on the utility of the module. In the latter case, an object would be an instance of the class of Volvos, like my 1991 Volvo 740, Vehicle Number VV1FA8843M2525801.

Object-oriented programming is far more complex than what I have just described. It has become the rage—perhaps, in part, because it *is* complex and raises the demand for programmers who excel in it. Today's programmers have taken to it. It is appealing because a programmer can absorb one program into another simply by referring to it. "You can crank out the code much faster," says Clinton.

Software salesmen will tell you that object-oriented programs, because they are derived from classes of objects, tend to be reusable. I'm not sure that they are any more re-usable than any other programs. In the November-December 1998 issue of *American Scientist*, Brian Hayes, in his article "Identity Crisis," explains that proving the equality of programs that modify the state of the computer is undecidable: "That is, there is no algorithm that will always yield the right answer when asked whether two arbitrary programs are equivalent. See Richard Bird's book *Programs and Machines*." If you are concerned about the reliability of re-used programs, consider that re-usability was invented by salesmen, not mathematicians.

Often, a "re-usable" module is not exactly what is needed. It might have to be shaped a little to fit some new application. The almost-right-but-not-quite syndrome applies to presentations as well. Throughout my career I have created hundreds of presentations, many of a general nature. I never re-used any of them without modification. The audience and the message varied just enough from one occasion to the next.

I spent most of the 1980s helping to manage proposals for large computer systems. I was a software salesman-engineer. I touted everything that came down the pike, from chief programmer teams to structured programming, to formal design, to CASE tools, to process control, to data models, to metrics, to Ada, and beyond. One of my last proposals was the Advanced Automation System. In IBM's proposal for the acquisition phase I touted "re-use"—although object-oriented programming was not used on the project.

I looked up the word *re-use* in the *Oxford English Dictionary*. It cites a reference from an 1843 issue of the *Civil Engineering and Architecture Journal*: "The water is to be re-used for forming the solution." Later, in 1865, from another source, "The fittings have been entirely re-used, and the carvings preserved." Here we have an example of the thing itself and of interfaces. Of course, there is no mention of re-using languages and symbols, no mention of rapid specialization, where one can add, modify, and delete abstract machines within seconds.

Computer programming is a bit of a miracle. With the click of a mouse we can generate new products almost overnight. Why, then, do we persist in trying to make it even easier? So developing software correctly is difficult. Developing vaccines and medications without side effects is difficult. But neither enterprise will benefit from shortcuts. Building a few re-usable templates so that we can, more quickly than ever, rush software out the door is simply contrary to the nature of programming. It seems that convenience and programming are not just related, they are in love with each other. So I should not be surprised that, when it's convenient, we would treat programs in opposing ways to suit our fancy: like the most ephemeral of objects, language, *and* like iron molds. Re-usability is popular now because we have discovered how hard it is to write correct programs and know it. Despite the miracle, it just takes too long, especially when there is so much we want to automate while we're still young.

I have some personal experience with re-use. When I was a kid in Gettysburg, I would walk with my father up the back alley that parallels Route 15, past the National Cemetery, to Gilbert's Hobby Shop. Mr. Gilbert sold model railroad gear. He also sold toys and bulk ice cream, which were of greater interest to me. The ice cream had to be spooned out of a tub into heavy paper containers, which on a hot day you could carry about two blocks before it melted and seeped out. So we would hustle back down the alley to Mom and Pop Troxell's cellar. They had the only freezer in the neighborhood. At that time, sharing was not uncommon. Neighborhoods shared: one television, one freezer, one phone line.

Sharing is one side of re-using; copying is another. Mathematicians distinguish between sharing and copying. The term *self-same* applies to one object, identified by one name, that can be referred to or used by many, like the freezer. The term *separate but equal* applies when there are two identical objects with unique names.

My first run-in with copying was on the IBM 029 keypunch machine. The drum could be programmed to duplicate certain columns and not others—to save keystrokes. I once copied a bogus card given to me by a prankster that caused dozens of errors and hours of wasted testing. In the 1960s and 1970s, programmers using IBM's System/360 copied what IBM called JCL: job control language statements. They referee a programmer's program and the operating system. We all learned who had the master JCL. To run your job, you made a copy and put some twist on it to suit your needs.

Card decks were copied, as were paper tapes, files kept on magnetic tapes and disks. In over two decades of programming, I mostly made copies—at all levels of conception, from the abstract to the physical.

Ah, those levels of conception! Alfred North Whitehead and Bertrand Russell would have a field day with computer programs. It seems to me that computer systems and programming attract brainy people because symbol systems mix abstractions. One thing appears to be something else depending on how you look at it: operators as values, values as operators, names as programs, programs as names, names as names, or names of names, programs as specifications for other programs, programs as models, models of programs,

programs as objects. A computer program can show up in any garb: as an artifact such as a calculator, as a specification for a calculator, as a model for a program that calculates taxes, as a specification for a model of a banking system, as a theory of arithmetic, as a model of a theory described in another program. The Universal Turing Machine, one of the decisive theories of twentieth-century mathematics, can be expressed as a program, as that program itself is an expression of computation, the very object of its theory. Before Turing, only scientists and mathematicians created theories, certified engineers and architects built models and created processes and specifications, and artisans created artifacts. Now anyone can create any of them by making a copy and changing a few symbols.

On the Advanced Automation System, by fiat, everything was re-usable. Iron molds abounded: the operating system; services written for one application that might be used for a second, or a third; specifications for files; application interfaces; supporting programs; programs in the first increment that would be executed in the second and successive increments; interface specifications; and, most important, shared code, code that many programs had to use.

I watched the saga of re-usability unfold. It was not long before important distinctions blurred. Was it better to have one copy and hold one organization accountable? Should copies be made of design specifications or of source code? or of object code, the executable image? Would it serve better to copy behavior or structure, or process? Would it not be better if the entire town of Gettysburg used Mom's freezer? Why have more than one? Suppose we inherit errors as well? Then what? They could spread like melanoma. What is the impact of the evolution of organizations on the evolution of processes, and of the evolution of processes on the evolution of programs? On the Advanced Automation System project, these questions were asked late or not at all. In assuming that more is better (or is it less?), all track was lost. Eventually, re-use, at first seen as efficiency, became an unholy dependency. In the project's salad days, it took a week to build the system. The programs were wrapped as tightly as a hangman's noose.

But re-use sells. After all is said and done, the Advanced Automation System may be remembered more for its role in the age of publicity than the age of computers. IBM made a small fortune on the project, despite its sad ending. As Harry put it then: "The most important piece of hardware on the Advanced Automation System is the overhead projector."

Journal Entry 84:

Programmers will always make errors. No advance in formal languages will once and for all prevail over human fallibility.

As near as I can tell, there are two approaches to software errors: one accepts them as inevitable and steers work toward removing the faults that errors produce; the other ignores errors, the resulting faults, and the failures they may cause, and replaces testing, discovery, and repair with legal and business maneuvers. (Great programmers, I am told, don't make errors—or they pale before the ingenious features they intrude upon.)

Man's greatest asset, and his greatest liability, is his knack for enduring. We struggle through the unwritten rules of four-way stop signs, ambiguous directions, airport delays, meaningless wars, chemical foodstuffs, physical and emotional pain at the level of ten, lesser pains like tedium, waiting in lines. Next to these, computer failures may not seem so awful. So far.

It is only a matter of time before we have to come to grips with the failure of automation on a large scale. Then politicians and economists and media pundits will shift their views, as they have with cigarettes.

We have less to fear from smoking and automatic weapons in the hands of children than we have to fear from automation running amok. But, as Bill Bradley writes, standing in the way of this technology is hopeless.

On the other hand, errors can be funny. Charlie Chaplin makes us laugh when he slips on a banana peel. I wonder if anyone has done a study of the relationship of errors to laughter?

If the rise of national socialism in Germany in the '30s and '40s was an error, then here's something to laugh about. When Clare Boothe Luce—who was covering the war in Europe—was advised by the concierge at the Paris Ritz to leave immediately, she asked why. The man answered, "The Germans are coming." She asked, "How do you know?" He replied, "Madame, they have reservations."

13
. . .

ERRORS

The greatest use of . . . pure reason is . . . a disci-
pline for the determination of the limits of its exer-
cise; and without laying claim to the discovery of
new truth, it has the modest merit of guarding
against error.

    —IMMANUEL KANT, *Critique of Pure Reason*

Rudolf Carnap, the great logician, after skiing with Ina near Pod Homolkou, sat at his table and wrote a formula. A strict man, he took no alcohol and no coffee and he did no science after dinner. Nevertheless, the splendid carving sitting atop the bookcase beside his table distracted him—perhaps something in the polished wood he so admired, or the memory of its acquisition—and he made an error.

Had Carnap been writing a computer program, his error, undetected, could become what professional programmers call a fault, or a logical sequence that produces a result other than that intended by the programmer. Some computer scientists have made a career of studying software faults. They are worth studying. The number of faults lying in wait within a software product or system is virtually unknowable. Many faults never cause a failure, or a loss of service of one degree or another. Many faults are never discovered, simply because portions of the software are never executed. Rarely, some faults offset others, rendering the entire logical sequence harmless. Some software is designed assuming the presence of faults; fault tolerance is built into the programs. The software recovers without causing a failure, like a right fielder bobbling a fly ball into the glove of the center fielder. No harm done; the batter is out.

The data I have studied, looking at project histories, suggest that a fault, once discovered, rarely turns out to be the work of a single operation, but is, more often than not, a logical sequence that runs to dozens of lines of code and crosses modules.

Defining failures is another difficult proposition. Every project should define what is meant by a failure as precisely as possible and, further, categorize them. Software systems and products should not be released until the failure rate is within the bounds acceptable to all users. And there should be no severe failures. It is reasonable to expect failures, even severe failures, but they should be masked by recovery mechanisms to prevent loss of service to the users.

Software is no less frivolous than the makings of an automobile or the workings of a hospital. In fact, software is the least frivolous product I can think of. For one thing, it is embedded in the automobile and the hospital, and in a thousand other safety-critical goods. It also stands on its own.

As Harry writes: "Failures in the new era of software, the epoch of Microsoft and the overthrow of the adult world by abstractions that edge toward the unnamed, even unnameable, are undefined, unfamiliar, and unfathomable, the kind not found even in the immense early systems that dwelled in simpler hives. These new failures are wild and enigmatic, the synthesis of speed and conceptual size, complexity and marketing."

He adds: "At the pace we are going, faults will become intractable. They will be pushed down farther and farther. Layer upon layer of programs will build on faults as they build on features. New programs, like paintings, are not new; they absorb old programs. Early versions, sometimes twenty or thirty years old, inhabit systems like fossils. Faults have become genetic, like oncogenes. It will be harder to get at them and fix them, because the programs nearer the surface, nearer to us, will obscure them.

"This is already so. In the new dawn, a single workstation weighs in at 64 million bytes worth of programming: operating systems, database management systems, networking systems, transaction management systems, this or that compiler's run-time support, file servers, security kernels, and a few applications. For a long time now, when a programmer writes a program, it is not written to the specification of a computer. It is written, in part, to the specification of the programs that preceded it. The earlier program's implementation is the latter's partial specification. With each passing year, the statement "A := B" will require more and more operations to work perfectly. This fattening may have an unfortunate side effect. How much time and money will be spent verifying the correctness of a fifty-statement program being added to a thousand or a million programs, to an ocean of programs, all beyond proof, many untested?"

Programming errors are becoming easier and easier to make. Distractions have increased in number and diversity as the world has become noisier. Lesser logicians than Carnap lose track. And we have come to rely too much on software tools to catch our errors, many of which are too subtle for automation to detect. Add to these the increasing size and complexity of software products and systems and the strenuous work of translating real-world automation into programs.

Now consider this. A new statute is being added to the Uniform Commercial Code to cover software: Statute 2B. The intent of Statute 2B is to define software not as goods but as rights licensed by the customer. The statute would allow suppliers to disclaim warranties. The draft language reads "This [information] [computer program] is being provided with all faults, and the entire risk as to satisfactory quality, performance, accuracy and effort is with the user." The customer would have neither refund nor lawsuit rights.

Sometimes failures are about the truth—no, most of the time. In his book *What Do You Care What Other People Think*, the physicist Richard Feynman, while investigating the causes of the 1986 *Challenger* disaster, asked IBM the same question he asked a dozen contractors in a dozen fields: Does your stuff have faults in it? IBM answered yes. IBM, Feynman later said, was the only company where the technical staff and management held the same view: that faults are inevitable and the entire company must commit to overcoming them. "The engineers and the managers communicate well with each other, and they were all very careful not to change their criteria for safety," he writes.

Engineers learn from failures. In 1965, a brand-new large computer system at Eglin Air Force Base caught fire. It was the Space Detection and Tracking System. The fire started near the punched-card drawer. Within minutes it swallowed one loop after another. The programs dissolved. Loads and stores and bit shifts flickered in the air. Some survived, but not enough. It didn't take long to discover that copies had not been made. The once promising system did not go up in smoke—it smoldered. Soon afterward, companies made daily backups standard procedure.

T.V. didn't wait for the company edict. He was at Elgin when the cards went up. After that, every time there was a fire drill, you would see H. (everyone called him H.—his full name was Thomas Vallon Harrison Boyce) hauling his seven or so boxes of cards down the stairs and out the side door to the secure area. He wasn't taking any chances.

After the fire, H. got funny about making copies. When the company bought cheap copiers that would chew up your work, H. wouldn't use them. For a while he'd ask the secretary to make copies. But then a couple of times she lost the package he'd given her. So H. stopped making copies altogether.

Later he stopped generating any paper, because he figured if you had paper, sooner or later you'd have to make copies, and since that was out, why get into it in the first place. He became Bartleby the Scrivener incarnate. He just "preferred not to." From then on H. just talked to people. Like Socrates, he wouldn't write anything down. He reasoned that if people had to write it down to remember, "it" wasn't worth remembering. H. said we need to learn how to put forth cogent logical arguments. It's a lost art, he said. Now we just talk louder. Because of the fire at Eglin, H. created a philosophy for himself.

C. A. R. Hoare has a strong opinion about programming errors, faults, and failures. Someday there won't be any. He describes the programming project of the future: "The description hardly makes reference to the most common feature of present programming practice, the programming bug. I have left it out because it won't exist. There will be no bugs. There will be no chance for a bug to germinate or to propagate. Every stage of the specification and design and coding will have been checked with mathematical rigor."

I'm not sure what Hoare means by "bug." Does he mean a fault, or a part of a fault, an operation, that in concert with other operations and variables and values could cause a failure? Does he mean a failure? Is he referring to the errors we make in creating faults? A word like *bug* should alert us that we are not dealing with science. (And Hoare is one of the most eminent computer scientists in the world.)

When I was a youngster, you could be sure that when the doctor told your mother you had a bug, he didn't have the faintest idea what was wrong. Was a bacteria involved? A virus? Could it have been that my immunological system was the problem? Maybe I just didn't want to go to school.

I'm also somewhat in the dark about what Hoare means by "checked." Something along the lines of a mathematical proof? Perhaps a set of symbols slightly larger than the program text, but not nearly as large as the proof of Fermat's Last Theorem? Something that would convince other parties that the program will end in a correct state for all possible executions, including those unintended? Hoare, of course, is imagining a world already out of control.

Most programmers hold a different view. They are not troubled by errors, faults, and failures. Harry writes: "Buggy code is cute and there is money in it. No one can make money in programming working like mad to avoid introducing faults, or working like mad to find and fix them. There's a limit, but, by and large, maintenance is where the money is. Early to market and future releases. There'll be no stopping the assembly line, not until companies are forced to."

Years ago I worked on a maintenance contract for the U.S. Navy. Revenues were measured in terms of the number of failures eliminated. The more code we fixed, the more money IBM made. (Sometimes programmers introduce a fault while fixing another. This is inadvertent and ordinary—part of the nature of programming. In fact, most of what programmers do is *fix* software.)

We usually know when software fails: the user makes a loud noise. In the worst case, programs just crash, as if they are tired or want to get away from it all. This is why safety-rated systems use backup systems. But if it's your PC, you've been trained to turn off the power and start over. In its office system, Microsoft recommends the following strategy to fend off failures in the print program: turn the machine off and on four times daily. After a rest, the computer and its programs may be just fine. Not always, though.

On any system, large or small, it also helps to shun certain features. After a while, you learn to steer clear of trouble, like in golf: the lake on the right, the out of bounds behind the green. You take an extra stroke to play it safe, or you just skip that hole.

Perhaps nothing reveals the nature of programming better than the so-called error message. Here is an example from IBM's Office Vision software: "CALLEUI failed with REXX syntax error 5 at line 1: machine storage exhausted." You know a lot of trouble was taken to perfect this product.

I was searching the phone directory for a man named Keyes, when this message spilled down the screen. I spelled his name "Keys." *Keys* is one of those words programs use privately. After a while you get a sixth sense about them. Like the slash (/), or the asterisk, or *log*. In most error messages, there is a to-whom-it-may-concern quality. In this case, it would have been timely to have a REXX source listing handy. Not just any listing, of course — *the* listing.

The next generation of programmers may improve upon this, not with careful programming but with more of it. I foresee this unwelcome shriek, "CALLEUI Failed . . . ," transformed into a cartoon, a graphic of a computer with short legs and three-fingered hands chugging pell-mell across the screen, sinking as it reaches the right margin, then flopping over on its back like a cat. We will become so amused that we will forget the failure. Certainly, it will be forgiven. We might even wish for an encore.

Journal Entry 100:

I read four newspapers a day. I don't watch as much television as I should. A friend tells me that I could learn a lot about the world watching the CNN reporters with the TV set on mute.

I was struck by one newspaper article yesterday. After several hours of testing, a piece of computer software will be used to grade aptitude tests. Not true or false questions, but reading comprehension. The software will evaluate students' essays and their arguments in response to verbal scenarios. I wonder how Cicero would fare? Was the software tested using excerpts from his *De Oratore*? I doubt it; except for the celebration of the Mass and a few prescriptions, Latin is dead. (A physician told me that Latin was used to communicate between doctors and pharmacists to ensure precision. Writing the name of a compound in Latin took some trouble, and that, it was believed, would reduce the number of errors.) Is Cicero—or his translator—guilty of dangling modifiers? How would Emerson and Thoreau do against this digital bar? And Lincoln? Did they occasionally skirt the topical sentence? Just what is the basis of excellence?

I have done some checking. Certain expressions are to be avoided: for example, "acid test," "breathless silence," "clear as crystal," "each and every," "holy bonds of matrimony," "in the last analysis," "slow but sure," or anything on the order of "Let me not to the marriage of true minds admit impediments." (Note: New evidence has surfaced that Shakespeare was not the bard of Stratford, but a woman, from parts unknown.)

There is much good about computers and the software that runs on them. Tools and techniques and technology are not new. Each step along the way they (we) have made our lives easier, more enjoyable. We have more leisure. We have more time to enjoy dinner and sleep, and to play and listen to the works of Bach or Ice Cube. We are into mining information, rather than coal, which is backbreaking. Some days, I like progress, some days not. I used to shovel coal into our furnace at six in the morning before school. I didn't like that. But I'm not sure I like our infatuation with what we call information, either.

14

• • •

THE ONE GREAT SYSTEM

It is difficult
to get the news from poems
yet men die miserably every day
for lack
of what is found there—
—William Carlos Williams

Harry wrote to me from Morocco: "Marie and I live near the ocean. We read a lot and take the train to the desert. I can think better with wheels under me." He wants me to rail around the globe with him.

Harry wrote that he had stopped drinking. I didn't know he had started. He spent a night in jail—some money trouble. I figure it was an argument with a waiter. Harry wanted everyone to do his thing perfectly.

In Morocco, in the cracks of living, Harry ruminated about responsibility—not his, but everyone's: "We spend most of our time dodging it." He considers himself an expert, although he can't define it. He reasons that responsibility lies on the other side of the circle from wanting something for nothing, or at least as little as possible. "It's an exchange. You give up struggling for worrying."

He met a Vietnamese man in Tangier, who got a college degree in the tunnels under the Ho Chi Minh trail. The man said he didn't want to cheat himself. Harry admits that in college he cheated on tests and cut classes to sleep—which may be the only ordinary thing about him.

The Ho Chi Minh trail was really a labyrinth of trails, a vast network we would call it today. West of the Mekong Delta, in Thailand, the United States maintained a surveillance facility that housed a number of IBM computers. Among other functions, the computers processed data from acoustical sensors dropped along the trail by American jets—a digital listening post. Infrequently, enemy traffic could be pinpointed. More often than not you could hear the Viet Cong hacking down a tree to get at one of the sensors. They would take it to the tunnels and puzzle over it. A friend of mine, Larry, who supported IBM there, told me that once in a while you could pick up the moaning of lovers in the tunnels, oblivious to the sensor's menace. Larry said we would have been better off—we might even have won the war—if we had dropped Chevrolets instead of sensors. It was a different kind of war, he said: "B-52s would drop their load on the elephants carrying supplies south." He quoted Robert Stone: "In a war where flying men pursue elephants, everyone just naturally wants to get high."

The IBM computers survived, sometimes by sheer luck. In 1970, it was decided to paint the metal barracks that held them. Vietnamese were hired, because their labor was far cheaper than that of the Thai locals. It was months before a helicopter pilot discovered the notation on the roof. In Vietnamese, it spelled "TARGET."

Harry's letters became more and more difficult. Usually, computers and programming figured in them. They were in the middle of his head. I think some major genetic aberration caused this. Harry's ideas eddied through his brain, like yours and mine do. But, sooner or later, his spun into the center, like water circling into a drain. There they worked themselves out through his obsessions.

Harry met a Sudanese man with whom he became friends. Around dawn on most days, Harry wrote, they would rendezvous at the man's apartment to discuss mathematics and programming and Alan Turing, and how Turing came to think of the schoolboy as "the computer" in his thought experiment that led to the Turing Machine. The Sudanese man would sit by his computer and stare straight ahead as they talked. Harry said he became afraid of him. Once, when Harry complained to him about his incessant smoking, the man threatened him. After a few weeks, Harry stopped seeing him. He learned later that the police were looking for him because of some letters he had written to the government.

Around this time Harry wrote that "I began to see the world differently." He says the Sudanese man helped him redefine himself. Marie wrote later that there were rumors. Harry also was growing very tired, so tired that he would stay in bed for entire days.

Harry saw the revolution coming, "the shift from a few people writing programs for large computer systems to millions writing *software*." In one letter he wrote: "In the last twenty years, programmers and their managers and sponsors have turned the stuff of mathematics into the stuff of beasts. In America, this has been veiled by layers of high-sounding terminology—so that it appears to be the stuff of archangels."

Harry liked to quote Gresham's Law: that intrinsically valuable currency, in circulation with debased currency, will be hoarded and thus driven out of the market. "Over time, the standards of goods, art, music, social conduct, will be lowered. Originality will diminish. Copying and forgery will increase and devalue taste and then meaning."

I received a note from him once with a clipping from the Sunday paper, an excerpt from Anthony Burgess's collection of essays *But Do Blondes Prefer Gentlemen?*:

We need some Johnsonian or Ruskinian pundit to frighten everybody with near impossible conditions for true creativity. We have to stop thinking that what kindergarten children produce with pencil or watercolour is anything more than charming or quaint. If you want to be considered a poet, you'll have to show mastery of the Petrarchan sonnet form or the sestina. Your musical efforts must begin with well-formed fugues. There is no substitute for craft. There, I think, you may have the nub of the matter. Art begins with craft, and there is no art until craft has been mastered. You can't create unless you're willing to subordinate the creative impulse to the construction of a form. But the learning of a craft takes time, and we all think we're entitled to short cuts. Art is rare and sacred and hard work, and there ought to be a wall of fire around it.

Scrawled across the top of the clipping Harry added: "Maybe we should build a wall of fire around programming."

Harry often repeated the theme of the one great computer system: "Soon there will be no mere handful of great computer systems. There will be *one*. One great system. We will be swimming in it like plankton, with no apparent shoreline, no reference point, no place to land, no home base. Generations down the road will wonder how they came to float upon this digital wave. Or they will take it for granted and think nothing of it."

Harry believed Marx was right that laborers will control the world—but through programming. "Programmers will join their programs to those of other programmers and these, combined, will ride across the sky, their loops on fire," he wrote.

Harry still thought of himself as a hardworking programmer. As he knew it, programming is hard work. Before he left the United States, he was involved in the union movement. But he got nowhere with programmers. They wanted to be left alone, or were too busy. But mostly, he once said, they felt they were above it all. Harry told me an experienced programmer, who routinely works 15 percent overtime and is not paid for it, makes less per hour than a machinist or a check-out clerk at the supermarket. He believed programmers should be certified, like professional engineers, and they should belong to unions: "Programmers on banking systems and space systems and communications systems and military systems are expected to make their schedules, even if it means working around the clock, or traveling here and there on a minute's notice. The best programmers are expected to do more and more until they take over the whole system. Too bad they are not paid by the module.

"The industrial revolution saw children working 15 hours a day, with punishment meted out for bad habits, like tardiness or dirty hands. As production increased and costs dropped, the tacit rules of labor became the norm, the new baseline. Factories made promises they could keep only if such conditions persisted. Programmers have become like these laborers. We cannot see them struggling on the line, of course, so it's all right. And we assume they love their work and are even obsessed with it. On the other hand, programmers should not be given special benefits and awards and perquisites and outlandish salaries. They should just be paid time-and-a-half for overtime."

Harry dropped out before programming found its niche in the world of adolescence, beyond unions, beyond professionalism, where you can clamber up the neck of a thousand loops and become a young man or woman of great wealth, where comportment can be journaled on a high-density tape and, using the strictures of set theory, eliminated as extraneous, where civilization can be boiled down to a few operands, where the culture of the street and the scientific merge like disparate cultures have met before, as they have met even in one human being, as happened with Rocca Secca of Acquino, the beloved Saint Thomas Aquinas, known then among his peers as the Dumb Ox, but who, unable to escape the inevitable marriage of ideas, brought Aristotle and the reason of Greece to bear upon the faith of Jesus.

Still, Harry would not have been surprised by this quote by Y. B. Kafai of the Graduate School of Education and Information Studies at California University at Los Angeles:

> There are currently few opportunities for children to go beyond button pushing and mouse clicking in their interaction with technology. By asking children to program software for other children, we are turning the tables and placing children in the active role of constructing new relationships with knowledge in the process. The most obvious benefit is that children learn about technology by building things of significance [sic], such as game software. But most importantly, through programming, children learn to express themselves in the technological domain.

(It's working. Already we have kiddie scripts called "exploiter" or "attacker" with names like "Smurf" and "John the Ripper," that enable children, with the click of a mouse, to penetrate the Pentagon.)

And further, Harry did not anticipate the often fruitless but nonetheless much-promised adaptation of computers and their programs to things far beyond electronic filing and arithmetic, to the collaboration of algorithms with men's and women's minds, and the rapture this would seed.

A friend told me of IBM's plan not to replace managers with computers but, rather, to form a partnership: "mind to mind." This happened in Australia. The Westpac Bank spent $150 million of a budgeted $85 million to "consolidate everything Westpac knows about the processes and enterprises required to create new financial products into a set of highly flexible software modules." The *IBM Systems Journal* article goes on:

> The factory would draw heavily upon expert systems and advanced software engineering that would combine bits of knowledge quickly at low cost in response to changing product and service demands. Information technology spun by knowl-

edge workers for mass customization. Knowledge workers are, after all, highly-skilled, customer-focused, self-directed, self-disciplined employees, performing complex, highly-specialized responsibilities that capitalize on their intellectual abilities . . . fostering team learning and system thinking throughout the organization.

Happily, the project was canceled. The bank later lost $2 billion. But there is more to come, as we edge closer to the apogee of abstraction, through purgatory and into cartoons. Cartoons, once used to sell software, have now become the product, each animated character a first principle, like the isosceles triangle, an animated dog barking directions to Avignon or the British Museum.

This is on the one hand. On the other, I ran into a man who works for the Coalition of Political Psychologists. He told me that, 15 years ago, some thoughtful political scientists and teachers and diplomats and arbitrators got together to bring the human element back into deciding the problems of nations. "It had become entirely numerical," he said.

Privately, Harry was thinking of a way to end programming as we know it.

GOVERNMENT PROJECT: SCHEDULE ALLOWS JUST ENOUGH TIME FOR FORMAL REVIEWS AND AUDITS; OF NECESSITY, HARDWARE AND SOFTWARE MUST BE "OFF THE SHELF" HUNDREDS OF CUSTOM FEATURES NEEDED BEFORE OPERATIONAL ACCEPTANCE

Journal Entry 104:

If you had asked me in 1965 who would become the greatest expert in programming and software development, I could have given you maybe five or six names. It would never have occurred to me that it would be the U.S. government, led by the Pentagon.

But the issue is still undecided. In the last decade or so, the private software companies, like Microsoft and America Online and Netscape, are giving the government a run for its money. In fact, in the mid-1990s, the government has yielded. They (or we) have tired of the cost of developing large software systems. We want turnkey solutions. But the nature of software will not be compromised. Software's utility lies in its specialization and adaptability, neither of which come cheap. So we continue to make promises to ourselves we cannot keep.

I would like to see standards for programming emerge naturally from the forces of education, like classical engineering. Today, there are very few colleges and universities offering degrees in software engineering. Schools that offer degrees in classical engineering demand academic excellence. Students must master mathematics and science and know how to apply them. Case studies prepare them for working in teams and organizations. Some engineering schools run their curriculum to five years.

Allowing bureaucrats and entrepreneurs to determine the course of computing and programming will, sooner or later, lead to disaster. I'm surprised a large-scale tragedy has not befallen us already.

More and more of us want to make money from this new form of technology. More and more of us want to participate in it. More and more of us are anxiously awaiting the next level of automation. More and more of us, within the field, worry about the state of current practice. But worrying and writing books and editorials will not make much of a dent. Even massive failures have not awakened us. Robert Danzig, our current and thoughtful Secretary of the Navy, writes of nonexplosive warfare (NEW). "A single computer virus, like its biological equivalent, can have widespread and proliferating effects . . . [it can] disable or distort the communications networks and other systems on which military and civilian life depend." Unfortunately, Mr. Danzig can imagine no better answer than "a new union of our public health, police, and military resources." I've always preferred an ounce of prevention.

15

. . .

THE GOVERNMENT OF PROGRAMMING

Government neither subsists nor arises because it is
good or evil, but solely because it is inevitable.
— GEORGE SANTAYANA, *Life of Reason*

The U.S. government, the administration and the Congress, is moving inexorably toward mouse-selectable, high-resolution graphical operations to control armaments, air traffic, tax collection, and law enforcement, to name but a few facets of our society. Harry: "We have gone way beyond push-button. War as war-*games* is not unthinkable. Vice President Albert Gore has a vision: all departments networked, controlled from a single, wired office, with a backup embedded somewhere in the Blue Ridge Mountains in the interest of fault tolerance. The invisible digital middle man, nameless, everywhere, but nowhere. Don't call your congressman; call the help desk."

In the 1980s and early 1990s, in the wheelhouse of the FAA's Advanced Automation System, government procurement procedures and regulations mushroomed. They mandated everything from contractor pricing to the number of "IF" statements that could be nested within one programming procedure. It seemed that, for every layer of complexity, a layer of supervision was added. (The government has recently swayed to the left, allowing private companies some freedom. But with the Year 2000 bug spreading fear throughout the nation—thanks to the rare collusion between the administration and the press—there may again be a shift to the right.)

Sometime during the mid-1980s, Harry had a dream that he interpreted as the government of programming. He wrote it down:

"I imagined a rope coiled on the floor tangent to and right of a crowbar. Imperceptibly, the crowbar moved across the circled rope, in small increments. I saw the generous area of the circle to the right of the crowbar as work, making a chair, or such. The area left behind, left of the encroaching crowbar: this was marked **the supervision of work** in bold.

"Then, thinking that the chair work was not going well, I moved the crowbar to the right, to get a better look. This done, the area of work decreased; the area of supervision increased. Less and less chair work was getting done. (Not just because the area is smaller, but because every increase in supervision taxes the work. Thermodynamically, more heat is exchanged.) I noticed that the work was still lax and I moved the crowbar farther to the right. The work area shrunk. The supervision area grew. I moved the bar to the right until work was crowded out and stopped dead."

There is a splendid course in the Johns Hopkins' technical management program called System Conceptual Design, in which students are taught the principles of designing large computer systems. Most of these systems are sponsored by the U.S. government, so the material draws heavily on the Department of Defense approach to building systems, military standards and all. The course case study is called "Improved Oceania Air Defense System." The name Oceania was chosen by the course authors, who believed it to be a mythical country. To set the record straight, there is an Oceania, and although it's not a country, mythical or otherwise, it is a place.

The real Oceania includes the islands of New Zealand and Australia, the Solomons, Fiji, Polynesia, and Hawaii.

Some of the fiercest World War II fighting in the Pacific theatre took place on or near these islands. There was Guadalcanal and the U.S. Marines. And there were the Fijians. Born and raised in the jungle, they became our most valuable scouts in the Solomons. They possess enormous strength, weighing in at about 230 pounds, with at least that much guile. Among the friendliest people on Earth, the Fijians were regarded with abject terror by the Japanese. Close in, the Fijians never lost in combat. They were as comfortable in what the Allies and the Japanese came to believe was hell as you or I would be in our hometown. Fijians knew nothing of air defense or systems. In over six years of fighting they relied almost entirely on knives and bludgeons, and had the fewest casualties per capita of any nation in the conflict. They love games, especially rugby. I'm sure the idea of a military standard document has never occurred to them.

"The more complex the work, the more we want to supervise it. That's why we have military standards," says the Major, who is now running his own large computer project. "We want new technology and that means software. And look at all the failures. We can't let that happen." On the phone, I once suggested to him that the projects that fail were meant to fail, that if we couldn't build a system, or use it, it wasn't meant to be, that governments, and especially democracies, move slowly, and that's OK. And too much automation before its time: maybe that's not OK. So things work out. "You know what that is," he said, and hung up.

The Major is a surefire kind of guy. He doesn't go in for probabilities. About 5'4" tall, he wears his hair just short of skinned. With whitewall temples, his jaw appears to run unbroken into the top of his skull, except for the metal-rimmed glasses he rams into his eyebrows. He walks like you-know-what: every inch the soldier. His favorite question isn't a question at all: "Do you receive my meaning?" He's a combat veteran. In countless battles, he has fought it out with Hughes, with TRW, with Boeing, with a lot of contractors building large computer systems. His father fought in the Balkans 50 years ago.

The Major is likable. He has quoted Thucydides at project reviews. I've heard he stands on his head for five minutes before lunch. He plays contract bridge and is quite good at it: a tournament player. Sometimes he "hypnotizes his self" doing needlepoint. He used to drag his needlepoint around with him, but never worked on it during meetings or on planes. The Major told me years ago he "played a key role in improving the quality of large computer systems by upping the level of supervision, because, basically, these prime contractors can't be trusted."

Who writes military standards? We do: the citizens, or a few government officials and subcontractors acting on our behalf. This is as it should be. We pay for these systems and they support us. And we don't take to systems that do not work. Standards need to be severe so that we can filter out those systems for which we have no consensus, or clear need, or that are too complicated to build and use. Sometimes they are filtered out while they are being built. These are often called failures by people who know how much money was spent on them or who lost out on promotions. But the systems are just being filtered later, after we've had a better look at them.

The real danger lies in successfully building systems that aren't good for us. So far, there have been only a few. Not that we aren't trying for more. Every week some new system or a new version of an old one is left to wither, its books stuck away in vaults, the code libraries purged. I wonder how many thousands of programs have been warehoused, left to some custodian. It's too bad we don't record the history of these rehearsals, scrupulously, like scientists. We could learn something. Maybe we would learn not to make the same mistakes, if mistakes are what we are making. But there is no provision for this, no journal of lost systems. The dead are not even named, just forgotten.

Governments and their subcontractors tend to specify the design of prospective systems in detail. There is a simple reason for this. Put any problem in the hands of an experienced engineer and he or she will continue to elaborate it until either the time or the money runs out. The more time and money allocated to the sponsor to define the system, the more likely it will specify how modules should be constructed, how tests should be run, to what degree the system should be distributed, and so on. The elaboration goes on in direct proportion to the number of government employees and subcontractors and the severity of the procurement policies. It is less apt to roll on when government streamlining is popular. When the elaboration rolls on, as it did on the Advanced Automation System project, it weighs heavily against the contractor's flexibility to modify the design. When the design details and the rules for designing are imposed by contract, common sense is replaced by litigation.

The practice of government-designed computer systems began early in our digital history. In 1963, the FAA insisted the automated en route air traffic control system use a multiprocessor—the 9020, as it turned out. It was believed to be the best way to protect against failures. IBM, one of the bidders, felt a duplex would be fine, one computer backing up another. A much less complicated solution, it would require no investment in a new computer. Very few multiprocessors were on the market then, and none met the FAA's requirements. Joe Fox, IBM's salesman for the project and a writer of children's books, met often with T. V. Learson, IBM's chairman of the board, about building a multiprocessor. Learson balked at the idea, but after many meetings he gave in. Fox assured him that IBM would not be in the air traffic control business without a multiprocessor. So IBM designed and manufactured the 9020, and wrote a specialized operating system to support it: the NAS Monitor. This took seven years. Custom-built, the 9020 and the NAS Monitor were never sold commercially.

The FAA wanted a commercially available multiprocessor that met the air traffic control availability requirements. Put another way, the FAA wanted to buy commercial products *and* it wanted them highly customized, in this case, for air traffic control.

For over forty years, the U.S. government has been specifying conflicting requirements—and changing them throughout the development cycle. This costs the taxpayers a considerable sum of money, and it is one of the reasons so many large systems fail.

If the give and take between the sponsor and the contractor is reasonable, and the system is not too large or complex, chances are good that our government-sponsored systems can be built on time and at a fair cost. Frequent communications and reviews are essential. No one can foresee how a system will unfold. No one gets it right the first time. The buyers and the users and the builders must look things over from time to time, especially in the beginning, before it's too late. Suppose I wanted to introduce baseball to Papua. I'd seen the game played once or twice and have a rough idea about it. But I don't know the rules, the exact dimensions of the field, of the ball, of the bat. So I write down what I know and ask three tribes independently to come up with the specifications for the game. Then I say: "I'll be back in three months for opening day." I'd likely get three different games, and none of them would look much like baseball.

Unfortunately, the give and take can become personal. Then, before you know it, the project runs away. Auditors are brought in. They drill into the layers of documentation, looking for errors. Every aspect of the project is briefed. This costs more money and dilutes the production of the vital materials. But it creates a mound of new ones: correspondences that explain and correct facts and impressions, volumes of rejoinders, reports, sometimes hundreds of pages long. Nothing is overlooked. A misplaced gerund might cause a satellite to fall from the sky. The recommendation: More supervision is required. Then Harry's dream comes true. A few more years go by and the cost for a single programming statement exceeds $1,500, and Congress wants to know why.

NEWSLETTER TO THE FACULTY

"The Boeing Company engages in both government and commercial business. About 80 percent of its total business (gross dollar volume) is commercial, about 20 percent is with the U.S. Government.

Boeing's contract and finance activities comprise about 3,800 people. Of this number, about 800 handle all commercial activities, while the other 3,000 handle the U.S. government business. The contract and finance administrative effort is seen to be about 15 to 1 for government work compared to commercial work of equal dollar value."

CAN MICROSOFT HELP?

The Major: "We can eliminate all of this overhead; it's silly. We must start using commercial software; it will reduce development costs."

Harry: "I've looked into the methods of some of the commercial software vendors. Maybe we *should* consider having Microsoft build our weapons and energy systems and the IRS system, the whole lot. We would save the taxpayers billions. Sure, there would be problems: maybe in the end the software would be driving the law. But who would know? I forget who said it, but it's been repeated often: the United States is a government of laws, not of men. Maybe we could amend that statement to conclude: . . . of neither laws nor men, but software. I pulled this off the Internet not too long ago.

'Over the past several years I have successfully developed a number of software programs and have observed several other software companies, some barely making it. . . . Exceptional software is almost always developed quickly by a couple people. . . . The single, most important thing is that the individual programmer needs to be given total responsibility and control of the programming, including its function. . . . When I as a manager disagreed with a programmer, and we could not agree to agree, the programmer made the final decision. . . . Eliminate project design and review as an exhaustive and rigorous process. Most of the design should occur as the program is written. . . . Monitor progress on the project by talking to the individual programmers as [code] is being written. . . . You must trust the developers on the project to create a good product. . . . Sometimes there are failures. The important thing is to fail quickly so you have time to find another approach. . . . Personally, when I wrote my first commercial program, I knew very little about application programming. I did no studies, research, or design, because I didn't have the time or money. I just started writing the program and six months later I was selling the best product on the market and doing several million dollars a year. . . . Developers must also feel free to say what they think to their supervisor. . . . Managers should be the best programmers; look at Bill Gates. He is an awesome programmer. . . . DOS 3 was written at Microsoft by six people in eighteen months. DOS 4 was written by IBM. It took them several years with 100 programmers. Yet DOS 3 is superior to DOS 4 and is still the DOS of choice. . . . There should be no overtime pay. An excellent programmer makes over $100,000 a year. An awesome programmer can make over $1M a year. . . . Use profit-sharing and bonuses to get awesome products. . . . Developers should each have their own office. . . . Eliminate the dress code. I have never met a programmer that did an even adequate job who wore a tie to work. I have met a lot of very good programmers who wore shorts and sandals to work every day. . . . Avoid meetings at all costs. . . . Writing software is a lot like writing a book. Almost anyone can write garbage; very few can write a best-seller.' "

The author's ethic is most apparent in his final statement: If it is not a best-seller, it's garbage. Accordingly, we must classify Primo Levi's *Survival in Auschwitz*, H.L. Mencken's *The American Language*, and the novels of Virginia Woolf as garbage.

GOVERNMENT TESTING:
NOT LOOKING FOR FAILURES, FORMALIZED

The government likes to conduct an official test, an acceptance test, near the end of a system's development. This began with the Department of Defense and has spread throughout the government. The acceptance test, or qualification test, is aimed at showing that there are no failures in the system, or that they are at least tolerable. In the process, the search for failures is sidelined.

Both the government and the prime contractor benefit from early acceptance. For the government, "acceptance" is a major milestone; often it is on record with Congress. The sponsor's promise to deliver a system to the people, to us, is fulfilled. The contractor is rewarded financially for meeting or beating this deadline. The sooner both parties enter what is called the maintenance phase, the sooner the pressure is off.

The intentions are honorable: to demonstrate that the private sector has complied with its part of the bargain, that it has met the terms of the contract. But in practice, with this objective looming on the horizon, no matter how distant, both parties, the sponsor and the contractor, shade testing toward acceptance. So much emphasis is placed on "qualifying the system" that the tough business of testing every aspect of the system, to find as many failures as possible, is compromised. Precious time and money are diverted.

The acceptance concept may once have made sense, when systems were hewed of cloth and steel, when materials, not yet worn by time and use, could be declared fit. In contrast, software is never completely fit; its only constant is the presence of faults and their potential to cause failures. Faults don't so much inhabit the material as suffuse it. In a larger sense, they define it. So, in computer systems, acceptance testing is anathema to both science and engineering. Testing should simply continue until all of the performance criteria have been met, including the failure rate.

The very existence of an acceptance test ensures that, sooner or later, there will be pressure not to find failures, to reconcile test scenarios and the system they exercise so that the system will "pass." Remove this concept and testers would pursue the discovery of failures with a vengeance, the way NASA and its contractors pursued them on the manned space systems.

On the Advanced Automation System project, the FAA put great stock in qualifying each requirement, not the system that is derived from the requirements (and many other variables) but each sentence describing the system's potential behavior. The approach turned into a massive, ongoing acceptance test. As a result, IBM had more than two hundred people writing test plans and procedures for what was called requirements testing. A single department, of about a dozen testers, was assigned to integrate and find failures in the system. Five years into the project's acquisition phase, after tens of millions of dollars had been spent preparing for the acceptance tests, the imbalance was corrected — somewhat.

Requirements testing is a subtle way of treating a nonlinear, unpredictable system as if it were a discrete symbol, like a number or a word. The potential and the actual become muddled. Requirements are natural language statements of intent, peppered in places with arithmetic. These are discrete and usually quite vague *representations* of the system as it might become. But the truth is that two teams writing requirements for the same system would describe them differently, and neither would get it quite right, simply because "right" cannot be known until the system is built. Surely you could tell a space system from a medical system. But any one of a very large set of possible statements could describe either.

Requirements testing is a little like trying to reduce crime in England by running a test for each line in the Magna Carta. In practice, rhetoric replaces the scientific method. As with mathematical proofs, the quest for "true or not false" soon turns into a party — a not very cordial party — marked by endless debate over whether this sentence or that sentence has been verified by this moment of behavior or that.

On the Advanced Automation System project, the floors sagged beneath the requirements test procedures. Each test step attained the status of a lemma, and the lemmas were not recyclable. Each step was notarized, as if the very land on which the computers rest were changing hands. IBM was pressed into a gargantuan effort. Tests were practiced over and over, always witnessed by the FAA. Then there are the pretest briefings and the posttest briefings, and their respective rehearsals. As each requirement was "verified," it was checked off, like soldiers entering boot camp. All this so that we could count the uncountable. But a subsystem with 99 percent of its requirements checked off could be unusable.

The FAA called this formal testing. The term *formal* in computer programming has come to mean using mathematical methods, such as reasoning. But on the Advanced Automation System, *formal* meant ceremonial. Ceremonies are among the things we expect to be perfect, like the perfect wedding. Considering the arbitrary phrasing of the requirements statements and their paucity in relation to the system's romping behavior and its uncountable number of states, . . . well, it reminds me of my father's neighbor's approach to raking leaves: leaning on the wash-line pole, rake in hand, pontificating, while the whole world marches by and leaves trickle across the sidewalk. Later, everyone is surprised when failures show up in the field and missiles hit schools.

AN INFORMAL CONFERENCE ON QUALITY ASSURANCE

Charlie, Roy, and I met at a café to discuss history. Charlie is an artist living in the northeast of Washington, D.C. He and his wife and two other couples converted a two-story elementary school into lofts. There, Charlie makes wooden figures when he is not renovating houses. Roy is an accountant who once caddied for Eisenhower. The talk got around to Dinger.

Dinger, a fraternity brother of Roy's, was once the fastest man in the East, at least the eastern part of the United States. Charlie had never seen Dinger run. Roy and I had, but we couldn't describe the indescribable. Dinger looked like Roy Rogers. He grew up in Maryland and played a little soccer in high school. But he had not run track before coming to college. I don't remember who talked him into sprinting, but I remember his first race. He wore sneakers and ran the 100-yard dash in 9.9. That tied the school record. Roy couldn't recall Dinger working out: "Fact is, he never trained. He could put down the beer with anyone. Somehow he never gained weight. He smoked. A friend of mine saw him tamp out a butt just before stepping into the blocks at Dickinson." Dinger never lost a race until the end of his career, at the Penn Relays. Along the way he set a lot of records. He ran the hundred in 9.4 and the 220 in 20.9 in 1967 on Mount Saint Mary's uphill track.

Partway through the history lesson we were joined by Tom, a programmer and a fierce apostle of W. E. Deming, a long-distance man if ever there was one. Tom started in on Dr. Deming and the quality and process movement, he called it. This bored Charlie, who wanted to talk baseball. Tom talked about zero defects and total quality management and six-sigma and the Malcom Baldrige award, all of which he said Deming abhorred but which many people think he started. This prompted Roy to contribute: "American pundits. They picked up on Mr. Toyoda's tactics—integrated teams, just-in-time delivery, continuous improvement, all aimed at increasing profit through conformity of labor, which leads to skill loss, lower wages, and downsizing through automation—then sold them to executives, who executed. Loyal lieutenants applauded the tactics, wrote articles extolling the pluses of efficiency, method, and automation, sped off to implement, and were among the first to be laid off."

Tom told us the story of the Ford Taurus in the early 1980s— how Ford, dating back to the McNamara years, relied on inspectors to find errors, cheerfully relieving the people on the line of any interest in doing their jobs well, and how, after losing billions a quarter, Ford turned it around with the Taurus by firing the inspectors and asking the workers at each station to take matters into their own hands—not only the quality of their work but how they did it. "Now this is just common sense," Tom said. "But the government and programming companies spend millions to get their processes certified by independent standards organizations and institutes like the one at Carnegie-Mellon. Dinger wouldn't win a race today. Ten or so process experts would be asking him who makes his shoes and how often he adjusts his starting blocks and if he documents it, and whether he smokes and drinks, and how many wind sprints he runs in training before he runs the quarter for endurance, and if his times are calculated to the hundredths of seconds. The fact is they'd fill up a hundred sheets and give him a grade and leave and never see him run. Which is a shame, because Dinger was something to see."

Roy added: "So the government is well intentioned. Why not let them supervise? Do you see these guys at America Online? They call one of their executives a chief programmer—Leonsis."

"Wasn't he the King of Sparta or something?" Charlie asked.

"This guy's the king of greed. He's after the surfers now," said Roy. He quoted Leonsis: "This isn't about surfers. It's about surf, sharks, and sex, and by sex I mean . . ."

"Hey!" Charlie got interested.

Tom: "Greenhouses they call them. They have one for hecklers. You log on and roast somebody—anybody."

"Sounds good to me." Charlie leaned in, as Tom, getting angry, puffed: "These guys are as disconnected from history, you know, culture, as that kid in Oxon Hill who shot a kid for his jacket. Two sides of the same coin. Somehow the DNA got lost."

I added: "We've always disguised ourselves, been one thing and faked another. Sleeping, eating, 'performing.' And then, oh by the way, humility. The bishops of Rome dress like women in simple gowns so no one will notice the ten miles of material up their sleeves in South America."

That put an end to the history lesson, and I had to leave anyway. I know the pain of good intentions gone wrong. Walking down the esplanade, I couldn't help thinking that we always set ourselves up so the best salesman wins. At least in the short run. And how lucky Charlie is to be making wooden objects in a loft with his two dogs and three cats watching his every move.

AFTER FIFTEEN YEARS OF PLANNING, DESIGNING, DISSEMBLING, PLANNING AND MORE DESIGNING, STAFFING AND SCREAMING, IT FINALLY ENDED

Journal Entry 111:

From what I know of it, the Advanced Automation System was a hallucination. Working on it must have been like squatting inside the folded flowers of a poppy plant, siphoning the opiates undiluted. Seductive from the outside, the inside is psychedelic.

A friend wrote, telling me that each day, when the immense parking lots filled up, you could figure $1M was being spent, just on labor.

He likened his time on the project to his tour in Vietnam. The men and women in charge were hanging on to good news for dear life. But the grunts, most of whom were too young to know the difference, navigated through the jungle as if there were no project, no plan, no mission. They were taken up with the details of skirmishes and small victories and small defeats. They knew nothing of what went on behind the lines. Many of them were in shock when they were escorted out of the building by guards, loyal IBM employees who had believed in its family attitude. Times were changing and there were suicides.

He said men and women stared wall-eyed at one another. Competition for parking spots ceased, and buildings, heretofore occupied on behalf of the grand mission, were leased to other companies. At the time, the IBM and FAA employees who had given their all to the project did not comprehend that they were on their way back to sanity. The hundreds of paid watchdogs moved on, but not enriched. They traveled business class to an untold number of meetings and squirmed for hours in hard-back chairs, sitting in for the money. At first they were resented, then pitied. They had nothing at stake, even if the stakes were trumped up. I can't imagine a worse way to make a living.

At the end, my friend sent me this: "There is a long curving stretch of road behind the AAS campus. The road borders one of the few remaining farms in Montgomery County, Maryland. Three or four generations of the Crown family make their home on what looks like a hundred acres. The son's house is a half-mile north of his father's. I've seen the sun set there, across the fields lying fallow, naked except for the stark outline of a combine. It is hallowed ground."

16

• • •

THE SYSTEM TO END ALL

I got lost, unable to follow the inadequate signs and
unable to read the map by the dim cowl light.
           —WALLACE STEGNER, *Crossing to Safety*

The FAA's Advanced Automation System project may have been the greatest debacle in the history of organized work. I hesitate as I write this. Many years ago, my father, near the end of his life, suffered from alcoholism. Fortunately, and with considerable courage and work, he recovered. But when he was in its grip, it was tough going. One of the trying aspects of alcoholism is that it is often visible and public. My father, more than once, fell down in the streets of Gettysburg and had to be taken home or to the hospital. In exasperation I once proclaimed him "the town drunk." A wise friend overheard my remark. She responded quietly: "Bobby, in this town, there are many, many people better qualified for that title than your father."

What do I mean by debacle? In the commonsense meaning of the word, the project was not a debacle: objectives not met, cost overruns, missed schedules. At its best, the Advanced Automation System project pulled together the public and private sectors to explore new technology, various design concepts, new programming techniques, the relationship between the business and technical aspects of large projects, among other elements. The project in fact did not meet its objectives, but that does not distinguish it from other projects.

No, the Advanced Automation System project was a debacle because it brought out the worst in all of us, the thousands who worked on it; because people believed in and worked feverishly toward objectives that could not have been met under any circumstances; because of its atmosphere, which was slavish and mindless. Except for a few individuals, we learned nothing from it. We will do it again and again, with other applications, other sponsors, other contractors, other nations.

In my view, the demise of the Advanced Automation System was no one's fault. Finding fault, if it has to be done, should be done by experts, like politicians and media pundits. There is and was nothing in the culture of the FAA, or of IBM, the two major organizations involved in the project, that would militate against success. I hold both organizations in high regard. Both have been effective and ethical throughout their respective histories. As for the individuals, if the two thousand or so people who participated in the project had been replaced, person by person, a dozen times over, it would not have changed the outcome. The same mix of intelligence, ambition, professionalism, motivation, arrogance, anger, and commitment would have prevailed.

I have been urged to write a comprehensive history of the Advanced Automation System project. Such a book would be useful—and lengthy—but it was not the book I set out to produce. This chapter is part of a larger story. As such, it summarizes the objectives of the Advanced Automation System project and its outcome, and, along the way, highlights a few of the hundreds of byzantine vignettes that marked it. These are set against the background described in previous chapters: the culture of Ada; the influence of size and technology and the shift toward workstations and distributed processing; the wish to automate as much as possible; the strict rules imposed by the government in the midst of rising commercialism, hyperbole, and expectations; the nearly impossible task of testing software systems; and, farther down the well, the elusive nature of software and its unforgiving complexity.

The FAA's Advanced Automation System project began in 1981, at about the time President Reagan dismissed 11,400 striking air traffic controllers. The timing was not incidental. President Reagan believed that, inevitably, computers would relieve mankind of the brute labor that has kept it from pursuing its dreams. Automation, he often said, would ease our lives, even solve our social problems, a belief shared with even more conviction by our current vice president, Albert Gore.

In 1981, at the dawn of airline deregulation, about 300 million passengers were taking commercial flights in the United States. It was predicted that the number would grow to more than 500 million by 1994. Today, more than 20,000 airline flights are scheduled per day. In 1997 the number of passengers exceeded 500 million. By the year 2007, more than 2 million passengers per day will be in flight. The number of jets in the U.S. fleet is expected to grow from 4,775 in 1996 to more than 7,000 in 2007. Add general aviation (more than 180,000 planes) and military flights, and you have busy skies.

On the ground, the air traffic control facilities are, and have been for some time, under stress. Most of the stress is borne by human beings. Surprisingly, the role of ground automation in air traffic control is modest. Not much has changed since the development of the en route 9020 System and the terminal area Automated Radar Tracking System in the 1960s and early 1970s. The air traffic controllers have often resisted automation. If you were to visit an air traffic control facility and witness, firsthand, the urgent and autonomic nature of ground supervision of aircraft, you would understand why. In no other job are judgment and quick reflex so entwined, more so than in neurosurgery, I suspect. Any change in the controllers' environment can be traumatic. Change is inevitable. But the world of air traffic control is as vulnerable to change as it gets. Change, if and when it comes, must be imperceptible. A slight shift in the position of a knob can distract a controller and create what the FAA calls an incident—when planes get too close to one another or to other objects.

Cognitive scientists would have a field day with air traffic controllers. At any point in time, controllers must simultaneously take the measure of the computer-modeled relationship among aircraft, racing along at over 300 miles per hour, talk with the pilots, and make inputs to the computer. The interaction of perception, judgment, and response appears to be almost automatic. For good reason, their job is always listed at the top of the most stressful professions.

Professionals they are. Controllers work six-day weeks. Despite the mandatory two breaks a day, some work what is called the "Quick Turn": 3 P.M. to 11 P.M., followed by a 7 A.M. to 3 P.M. shift. These are the young tough guys who hug those planes and passengers to their bosoms. Others, often burned out, will take only light loads. But no one works the boards for long.

The alarming growth of air travel and the firing of the controllers were not the sole motives behind the Advanced Automation System. There was a more practical issue: the equipment—radars, navigational aids, computers, cables, telephones, the entire constellation—was, and is, getting old. The favorite word among members of Congress and critics of the FAA, such as Mary Schiavo, is *antiquated*. Even the software was old, some said, who do not realize that old software is more reliable than new software.

The FAA claimed that the major driver was financial. The FAA, whose mission is two-sided—it both supports air travel and supervises its safety—has been under pressure from the airlines to upgrade the computer algorithms to permit preferred routes of flight, which could save each airline millions of dollars in fuel. (According to the major carriers, today's rigid procedures, based on fixed airways, derived from a decades-old topology of ground navigational equipment, causes more than 20,000 delays every day, and wastes $5 billion a year. The advent of satellite navigation makes off-airway flying potentially more profitable.)

On the public side, the FAA wanted to dramatically reduce its operating costs. With the Advanced Automation System, most, if not all, of the terminal and en route facilities would be consolidated. The existing facilities would be combined into some thirty or forty area control facilities. Shutting down more than a hundred TRACONs and en route facilities—which means uprooting people, laying some off, retraining others, redirecting communications lines, renovating security operations, you name it—would, in time, save an estimated $4.5 billion in operating costs.

Technology was to play an important role in the consolidation. Computer equipment and software would be developed or purchased that could support any and all of the combined air traffic facilities and services. For this reason, the new controller workstation was called the "common console"—it could be adapted to any type of air traffic management: terminal, en route, oceanic, flow control, weather, even the management of the computer system itself.

The age-old argument favoring the advance of technology held true: efficiency, less toil and hardship, and cheaper goods blend as one. On paper, the plan was appealing. The investment to reduce the air traffic control system to its lowest common denominator looked as if it would eventually pay off. But there are always hidden costs: in particular, the displacement of people and jobs. The computer age has been especially effective in this regard. Between 1980 and 1994, more than 40 million people in the United States were laid off, displaced, retrained, or forced into early retirement.

The biggest problem in creating a new version of an old system is the transition. The air traffic control system operates all day, every day, and any change must be made while the system is running. I never saw a clear concept of how this would be done. The mission was laid out to make transition, at best, awkward; at worst, implausible. Contrary to the sensitive character of the air traffic control system, and especially the people who support it, the new system would be revolutionary, as radical a departure from well-worn mores and customs as the overthrow of the czars. Someone must have suspected as much, for there were advertisements to the contrary. The Advanced Automation System was touted as a model of the evolution of systems. In fact, there was one incremental phase in which the en route controllers would get new displays. This was evolution feigned. In the main, the system was designed to sweep away the old and replace it with the new. Technologists prevailed. A subtle and fragile culture would be transformed. By 1998—the planned end date for the project—the modus operandi of air traffic controllers, maintenance engineers, computer operators, guards, secretaries, and supervisors would become a rumor, the stuff of anecdotes. Where they had been and what they had done would be obliterated.

THE OBJECTIVES

The Advanced Automation System project spanned 14 years, from 1981 to 1994. Billions of dollars were spent on it. The project was "terminated for convenience" by the government. Maybe part of the problem was the name. There is more than a touch of hubris in calling a project the Advanced Automation System. What would we call the next one? I suspect its inventors could care less; they would be long gone by then. For them, it *would* be the culmination of systems. Their names would be affixed to it, and then they would die in dignity, knowing that they had created the system to end all systems.

One engineer I know described the AAS this way. You're living in a modest house and you notice the refrigerator deteriorating. The ice sometimes melts, and the door isn't flush, and the repairman comes out, it seems, once a month. Then you notice it's bulky and doesn't save energy, and you've seen those new ones at Sears. The first thing you do is look into some land a couple of states over and think about a new house, combined with several other houses of similar personality. Then you get I. M. Pei and some of the other great architects and hold a design run-off. This takes awhile, so you have to put up with the fridge, which is now making a buzzing noise that keeps you awake at night. You look at several plans and even build a prototype or two. Times goes on and you finally choose a design. There is a big bash before building starts. Then you build. And build. The celebrating continues; each brick thrills. Then you change your mind. You really wanted a Japanese house with red-wood floors and a formal garden. So you start to reengineer what you have. Move a few bricks and some sod. Finally, you have something that looks pretty good. Then one night you go to bed and notice the buzzing in the refrigerator is gone. Something's wrong. The silence keeps you awake. You've spent too much money! You don't really want to move! And now you find out the kids don't like the new house. In fact, your daughter says, "I hate it." So you cut your losses. Fifteen years and a few billion dollars later, the old refrigerator is still running—somehow.

On the Advanced Automation System, virtually everything was to change. Each air traffic controller would have his or her own workstation. He or she would operate an ensemble of computers and communications channels, software and peripheral devices, all hidden away inside the cabinetry. The workstation, the common console, was the showpiece of the new system. A 20" × 20" Sony display would bring high-resolution graphics to air traffic control; and each controller could tune the splendid graphics to suit his or her situation and preference.

The original TRACON and en route computers would be replaced. There would be new algorithms. A new digital voice system was coming along. The latest in fault-tolerant computing—algorithms to protect the air traffic control algorithms—would be installed so that the system would (almost) never fail—three seconds a year. (Later both MITRE and the FAA admitted that this was not achievable.)

There were many extreme requirements, any one of which could undermine the successful implementation of a digital system. Here is a sample: recording video by sending computer files over a local area network, because today's VCRs cannot handle the load presented by the huge Sony displays; replacing paper terrain maps with electronic renderings whose geographical markings could not be accurately certified; cutting over from one version of software to another while the system is running; distributing the processing of a single flight over dozens of computers whose synchronization could be undone by a single failure; replacing paper clearances ("flight UAL22 is cleared to altitude . . .") with electronic notes, coupled with the complete removal of printers (the FAA was zealous about having a paperless system—this system designed upon glaciers of paper). Deprived of old habits, the air traffic controllers would have no choice but to adopt new ones. A training system was designed that was to simulate the entire system within one workstation. Then there was a requirement for an entire air traffic control center to back up any or all centers, which might have required supercomputers not yet imagined, embedded in each workstation.

THE PROJECT

The project was conducted in two phases: a design competition, which ran from 1983 to 1988, pitted IBM against Hughes; and the grand prize, the acquisition phase. The design run-off included prototyping and the development of detailed plans and specifications, very few of which made it through the acquisition phase.

In the design phase, years before programs would be written, years before a contractor was chosen, specifications for computer programs were written to the bit level. Systems engineers worked 100-hour weeks to develop 1,000-page specifications for programs whose loops would begin to unfold in about seven years. (By then, the original specifications had been rewritten many times.) The software design was also to be completed in the design phase. It was believed that writing the design in Ada would make coding easier. But the programmers, unschooled in the use of abstractions, delivered what amounted to code in the design phase. This was even touted by IBM, which proudly proclaimed that it had written a million lines of Ada design. Virtually none of it survived.

The FAA later admitted that the design competition, which cost the taxpayers $1 billion, was of little value. Nevertheless, it was an opportunity for the private sector to advance. Hughes and IBM brought on their experts, people who, in the prime of their careers, had helped put man on the moon, had built weapons systems, had been heroes of another age in air traffic control automation. This was to be their greatest accomplishment, an accomplishment they would share with the dozens of subcontractors the FAA hired to watch them. Throughout the ranks, from top to bottom, in both the private and public sectors, this would be their finest hour.

Things began to go wrong almost immediately. By 1986, it had become clear that the consolidation of facilities was never going to happen. It is hard to believe that anyone ever thought it would. Yet the FAA pressed on. Just before the start of the acquisition phase, they decoupled the TRACON and the en route systems. But by then both contractors had conceived a design that embraced both. The mission had altered, but the technical approach went forward as if it had not.

The competition ended in 1988. Hughes, having taken on many of the characteristics of its founder, Howard Hughes, who brought a Hollywood approach to the aerospace business, predictably outscored IBM's proposal. But IBM won the job, because it was the low bidder, and because of IBM's long-standing collaboration with the FAA. Hughes protested, but its protest was denied.

At $3.7 billion, the Advanced Automation System was one of the largest civilian computer contracts ever let, maybe the largest. It was the largest single contract in IBM's history. From the moment it was awarded until near the project's end, IBM patted itself on the back. The efforts of thousands of people in the design competition phase fueled a years-long celebration. There was something for everyone, beginning with a great ball in Union Station, featuring Chubby Checker and "The Twist."

At its peak, the project employed more than two thousand people—about $1 million a day. If you thought like IBM's Federal Systems president, Gerry Ebker, this was a good deal. Many people were working and money was being made. No one considered that it would not last forever. In the meantime, everyone was getting ahead. (One of the ironies of conceptual work is that it is easy to believe you are farther along than you are; only symbols are being produced.)

Bugs in the Program, 8/3/89

A Report to the 101st Congress on problems in federal government computer software development and regulation, submitted by the Subcommittee on Investigations and Oversight.

Dear Mr. Chairman:

The Comptroller General reported in 1986 that the FAA Advanced Automation System—the foundation of the nation's ability to manage future air traffic—was being developed with an approach that does not adequately mitigate technical risks. . . . The program has already encountered significant cost growth (at least 50% in the design competition phase).

What may finally force a redefinition of this procurement system is continued failure to balance the budget. The strange policy where the Government pays twice for a system—once to buy it and again to make it work . . . cannot be sustained in an era of multibillion dollar shortfalls in the Treasury.

Behind every successful software system, be it air traffic control or medical diagnosis, is a software manager. Like software itself, these managers must be developed.

Adaptive intelligence in safety-critical systems may be beyond the capability of regulatory agencies to certify.

Nothing recommended in this report will have any effect on the software problem.

The Advanced Automation System project lasted longer than the siege of Troy, by four years. The story, as at Troy, lies in the effort itself. If you want to get a feel for how it was, you can read *The Iliad.* There, for example, you can learn in Book II:

> From the camp,
> the troops were turning out now, thick as bees
> that issue from some crevice in a rock face,
> endlessly pouring forth, to make some cluster
> and swarm on blooms of summer here and there,
> glinting and droning, busy in bright air.
> Like bees innumerable from ships and huts
> down the deep foreshore streamed those regiments
> toward the assembly ground—and Rumor blazed
> among them like a crier sent from Zeus.

As at Troy, the project struggled from one crisis to the next, always under the watchful eye not of gods but of FAA managers and the subcontractors hired to assist them. As the system grew in size and complexity, and the requirements drifted and expanded, the supervision escalated. Whatever commitment and discipline there was—and I believe all involved, both in the FAA and in the private sector, were deeply committed—was worn down by a battery of watchfulness that I can only ascribe to a fear of failure. Despite the tens of millions of dollars spent on new computers for the AAS, the most important piece of equipment on the project was the overhead projector, as Harry pointed out.

The project bellowed. The roar was deafening. Imagine trying to work out a tricky math problem in the front row of a rock concert. One programmer described it this way: "Working on the project was like working on a car inside the garage with the motor running. Eventually, even the crickets hopping around the tires suffocate." I wonder if we would have finished the original 9020 System in that environment? Or a spreadsheet program?

What I saw on the FAA's Advanced Automation System would make Sisyphus weep. In *Bullfinch's Mythology* Sisyphus' life in the "infernal regions" is described: "his task was to roll a huge stone up to a hill-top, but when the steep was well-nigh gained, the rock, repulsed by some sudden force, rushed headlong down to the plain.

Again, he toiled at it, while the sweat bathed all his weary limbs, but all to no effect."

The Advanced Automation System project gave life to MIL-STD 2167, the spirit of which opens the gates of software's third epoch. I cannot resist elaborating on it further. If you could sit down for an hour and imagine everything you might want to know about a system and its programs, in advance of their production, and write it all down in a contract, then add it to the list of 100 of your friends who were asked to do the same thing, you would fall short of the requirements for workmanship and documentation levied on the project. For every line of software, 100 pages were written about it. On such projects, hardly anyone programs. One test plan I saw ran to 800 pages to test five requirements for gathering online performance data. And when it came to something as important as system availability, the documentation scaled up. None of this was done once; it was done many times. Scores of people were paid to review and critique the work, which they did with glee. Every decision resulted in more work.

Government Computer News, 8/21/89

FAA MANAGER BLAMES IBM's Ada TOOLS

The FAA program manager, Michael E. Perie, said last week that immature technology in the Ada Programming Support Environment supplied by IBM has delayed the AAS.

IBM officials took issue with Perie's remarks: "Our APSE does not impact the software development schedule."

The FAA also has had some "requirements questions" regarding the contract, Perie said. "And we're still wrestling with how big that problem is in terms of schedule and cost."

IBM officials disagreed: "We're confident that if we encounter any early delays, that those would be overcome by progress made later."

Some of the software development problems "are just classic," Perie said.

Datamation, 12/11/89

FAA TO ASK REVISION OF IBM

Last summer, IBM stumbled on the third of seven builds. IBM has indicated plans to extend the fourth build from three months to six while adding one month to builds five through seven, Mullikin said.

Build four, Mullikin said, also will be lengthened to allow IBM to rehost software from the [*sic*] its next-generation RISC processor. The original schedule did not allow for rehosting.

Electronic News, 9/3/90

FAA PROJECT FACES MORE DELAYS

The FAA's $3.5 billion air traffic control program, already 13 months behind schedule, will likely be further delayed another nine months according to a recent report by the Government Accounting Office. "The 13-month extension does not consider the time required to resolve remaining requirements," the GAO report concludes. "Further, little time has been allotted for resolving problems that may arise from system testing."

LIFE ON THE PROJECT: THE 475TH EXAMPLE

Subject: In your mail (in reference to Harmon's mistake):

In your mail you will be receiving a copy of a letter from Riebau to Dennis Trippel. The letter expresses a concern that IBM is modifying PU10 without FAA approval, namely by changing STNs (Software Technical Notes) that are fulfilling PU10 DID requirements. The letter requests Trippel to notify IBM that the applicable STNs are frozen and that any changes have to be formally submitted to the FAA for review and approval—and that exceptions must be formally submitted via the deviation and waiver process. I will be working with my representatives to determine what ramifications this may have on the mechanism that we already have in place for getting FAA approval for STN changes. I hope that whatever we work out will be little to no impact on our internal process of STN change.

Have a nice day, Jenny

In 1991, Harmon, a lead programmer, convinced his team that the author should read his or her own source code aloud at inspections, not have it read by a disinterested party, as the procedures required. Harmon wanted to reduce the overhead of inspections, which had become grossly overattended and overdocumented. "Bloated," he called them. "They were interfering with the natural pace of programming."

The streamlining paid off at first. Programs in his area were getting done on schedule, and they worked. There were a number of reasons for this, but he attributed his team's success to leaner inspections. He was also an honest fellow, so he reported the new method to his quality assurance department, hoping to institutionalize it. Shortly thereafter they reported it to the FAA quality assurance officer. This was in keeping with the rules of quality assurance. The contractor may define his own procedures, but, having written them down, the contractor and the sponsor quality assurance departments collaborate to penalize any violations. There were no exceptions.

In about a month, the FAA wrote a letter to IBM insisting that IBM had violated its commitment to the very methods IBM had created. This could result in a reduction in fee. There were several meetings involving the FAA's quality assurance officer (Riebau), the contracts officer (Trippel), IBM's software development manager, IBM's director of development, and scores of others. No one could agree. The matter was escalated to Mike Perie and Bill Carson, IBM's vice president for air traffic control systems. Here, things were clarified. The system development plan, delivered with the proposal, was considered part of the contract. And the hundreds of standards and procedures developed along the way, riders to the plan, were likewise contractually binding. Unhappily, IBM was in breach of the contract because a programmer had given voice to his own code. After many more meetings, IBM apologized. Harmon was reprimanded, but legal actions were avoided.

My guess is that this episode cost the taxpayers hundreds of thousands of dollars, while projects by the hundreds around the planet were not using inspections at all.

A TECHNICAL PROBLEM

The Advanced Automation System came along about the time that mainframe computers and centralized processing were giving way to workstations and distributed processing. The diminishing size of computer chips, the speed of networks, and the improved resolution of graphics converged. There was no conspiracy behind this cocktail; it just happened.

When new technology becomes available, however it may be packaged, we want to use it. In computing, the sudden shift in size, speed, and imagery had an immediate and profound effect. Distributed processing became a given, even when it was not appropriate. Upgrading systems meant redesigning them. What might have taken a year or two—to replace a mainframe or add some software— would now require five to ten years.

There is nothing intrinsically good or bad about distributed computing. But giving form to a system—or anything, for that matter—that does not fit its intended behavior is very risky. We could still play baseball if the ball were shaped like a cube, but the game just wouldn't be the same. We could play soccer on a field 1,000 yards long, but the scoring would be quite low, and we'd have to tear down a lot of stadiums and build new ones. Or people would just have to stand to watch soccer. We could give every basketball player his or her own basketball and see how that would work. Such an implementation might well spell the end of passing. New architectural models can be insidious.

To a large degree, we now live in the age of distributed computing. We work at home on our PCs and send messages over the Internet, or read the Kenneth Starr report, the latest and grandest digital pornography, describing the president's sexual techniques in detail, before he or his attorneys have had an opportunity to fully examine the text. (Was this what Vice President Albert Gore had in mind for the information highway that he has proclaimed so loudly?) The issue is not distribution of data but the degree to which one computer's data need another's to perform a single calculation.

Each common console on the Advanced Automation System embedded two computers: one, a general-purpose computer, an IBM RISC/6000; and the second, a display generator, driven by a Motorola processor. It made perfect sense to program each console so that the individual air traffic controller could adjust his own windows and font sizes. This would have little, if any, impact on his neighbor, just as I can control the display and data entry particulars of my personal computer at work without disrupting a colleague down the hall.

The design of the Advanced Automation System did not stop there. Virtually all data were distributed: aircraft tracking data, flight data, diagnostics data, configuration data—all inputs, algorithms, and outputs. Theorists, hired early in the project, made convincing arguments that to achieve maximum fault tolerance, to achieve maximum availability, no computer should contain more data than another. The reasoning went like this: If one computer reigned over the others, and that computer failed, the entire system would be compromised. The other side of the coin is not as easy to explain.

On the Advanced Automation System, the other side of the coin meant developing, four or five times over, software that would keep *several hundred* computers' clocks synchronized, that would ensure that every calculation in every computer was correct, coherent, and consistent with respect to the entire constellation of computers, and that any failure in any one computer would not jeopardize the system's accuracy and responsiveness. The high-availability software ran to hundreds of thousands of statements. To get the few hundred thousand, millions of statements were written and rewritten, tested and retested, for over ten years.

To take a simple example, let's assume we want to calculate a point in space. The point depends on the coherence of four values defined as the variables: X, Y, Z, and T. The latitude, the longitude, and the altitude, accurate to 100 feet, and the time, accurate to a tenth of a second. There are three computers: one calculates X, the second Y, and the third Z. Their clocks must be synchronized to within 20 milliseconds. If any of the values is incorrect, missing, or calculated too early or too late, or if the protocols that send the messages containing these values from one computer to another fail, the result may be incoherent (for example, a point in space defined only as X and Y), incorrect, or inconsistent. There is another constraint: If this calculation fails for any reason, does the user of the result care? Do lives depend on the result? Or can the user, be it a machine or a human being, tolerate some error? If errors can be tolerated, to what degree and under what conditions? We may have covered 100,000 customized Ada statements with this example. In fact, no calculation on the Advanced Automation System was this simple. So make that 300,000.

Implementing the protocols to support this degree of fault-tolerant distributed computing was the programmers' greatest achievement. Nevertheless, when the project was terminated there were still problems. Once in a while, the computer calculating the altitude crashed and could not recover in time, because the load on the local area network increased the intercomputer latency. The result showing up on the air traffic controller's screen would be unpredictable. The altitude might be the altitude from the previous calculation, or it might be complete nonsense. Over the years, I would observe tests and notice that the many instances of the altitude of one aircraft, spread across various workstations, would not match. I calculated that, *inside* the computers, there may be dozens of instances of the altitude, in ASCII character format, as an integer, in EBCDIC character format. What were the odds, I wondered, that they were all the same at any point in time, given that computers would routinely fail and recover, bottlenecks would occur, clocks would drift?

A computer's failure and recovery is an example of a tactical transition: the phenomenon occurs immediately. The most devastating technical problem on the project was never solved: the strategic transition. Because the system was completely fault tolerant (at least in theory), there would never be a startup or a shutdown. The system was always running, like the Mississippi River. Computers could be switched in and out, reconfigured, subsystems partitioned, functions turned on and off, or run in degraded mode, but there would be no stopping the system.

The problem was how to cut over to new versions of the software while the system was running, especially with the elimination of printers. (Printers offer the users some opportunity to continue controlling airplanes even if the worst happens and all machines go down.) The FAA management was adamant about no printers. The Advanced Automation System was to be an all-digital, perpetual computing machine.

New software versions are always coming along, containing fixes or new features. Their insertion into the operational suite can be an intractable problem when no part of the work is captured on paper, or when no completely independent digital backup system exists. If the work can continue elsewhere, computers can be stopped for a while, reloaded, and resynchronized, and new programs reconciled with old values. This was not the case on the Advanced Automation System. Reconciling would mean writing additional programs to remap the version 1 values to fit the operations of version 2. In the worst case, this "transition" software could be as large as the operational software being upgraded. It would also have to be tested and certified and downloaded and executed during air traffic control operations.

Many analogies were used to describe the cut-over problem. "It's somewhat like replacing the engine on a car while it is cruising down the turnpike." It took five or six people, FAA and IBM, over a year to convince thousands of others, including the FAA and IBM project managers, that dynamic cut-over of software could not be done in any reasonable way. But then it was not long before everyone was an expert, proudly characterizing his or her version of the obvious. One of the early FAA project managers used the car analogy in the *Washington Post* long after the project was terminated—hindsight drilled into his central nervous system masquerading as insight.

A PSYCHOLOGICAL PROBLEM

It was noted by everyone from the *New York Times* to the vice president of the United States that the main problem on the Advanced Automation System was "changing requirements." For those involved in large-scale computer systems, that is nothing new. No one can perfectly surmise the shape and feel of a system years in advance. Even when you're replacing some aspect of a system you know by heart, you must stop and think about it, twice, three times, or perhaps a dozen times.

But the requirements churn on the Advanced Automation System project was not normal. It was the result of our enchantment with the computer-human interface, or, as we called it, the CHI. The common console, fronted by the Sony 20" × 20" color display, was capable of a seemingly endless variety of presentations. The design of the display software, and its outputs on the screen, mesmerized the population of the project like the O. J. Simpson trial mesmerized the nation.

From top to bottom, everyone was charmed. So, in large part, the project was handed over to human factors pundits, like Sydney, whose favorite movie is *The Maltese Falcon*.

Thousands of labor-months were spent designing, discussing, and demonstrating the possibilities: colors, fonts, overlays, reversals, serpentine lists, toggling, zooming, opaque windows — the list is too long for this summary. Virtually all of the marketing brochures, produced prematurely and in large numbers, sparkled with some rendition or other of the common console and its CHI.

For Sydney, the Advanced Automation System was to be a lifelong research project: Over and over, on and on, what the user might do, or could, or would. What might this controller think in that situation? How might . . . ? What if the night . . . ? We all got into it. It was fun — at first. There were lots of demonstrations and photography sessions with users' smiles reflected in the workstation glass. As the CHI blossomed, so did Sydney. He was in tight with the FAA and IBM's senior management.

Not everyone loved Sydney. If he did not prevail on the minutest point, he would sulk, prance, or fume in a rage. It seemed that the more bellicose he became, the more he was rewarded — first one promotion, then another, then a third. He would back people into a corner and shake his fist at them. He would beat on filing cabinets. Then he would get an award.

After years, the requirements began to converge. Sydney took to sitting in his room in the dark with a blanket over his lap. He worked like a demon to dredge up new wrinkles. He would scream in meetings and pound his fist. The executives shrugged. Sydney knew the end was coming. Computer programs would have to be written. His eyes would flash. Then he'd make a joke. Some laughed uneasily. They were afraid of him.

When the design of the CHI was done, Sydney was a wreck. So was the project. The seemingly boundless array of commands and displays became a feeding ground for writing failure reports. Preferences became failures. "Human factors," muttered the software development manager. She couldn't understand it. When she had begun her career there was no such thing. "It's like finding fault with the weather. One day it's too warm. Then it's too cold, or windy, or muggy." The failure reports mounted in proportion to the CHI requirements. The air traffic control algorithms were almost forgotten. So was the budget. "We're in too deep now," said the IBM project manager.

Near the end, Sydney became morose. He began meeting with one of his associates in the front seat of his car. Everyone knew they were discussing the CHI and how to improve it. Sydney now saw that everything was wrong. Despite his efforts, his foresight, and his genius, the wrong things had happened. No one had listened. No one knew what he knew. He and his associate would sit in the car all morning. Then all afternoon. Sydney had hoped a monument would be raised to him on the avenue. Instead he was laid off.

(In retrospect, it may be that we were able to field the original en route and TRACON systems within a reasonable time because, on the front end, in development, we could use only punched cards—there were no CASE tools—and our programs produced data for mechanical equipment and displays that operated much as they had in the 1950s: no human factors analysis; no indecision. We could concentrate on the arithmetic, which was difficult enough.)

The cost of what turned out to be a 14-year human factors study did not pay off. Shortly before the project was terminated, an air traffic controller on the CBS evening news said: "It takes me twelve commands to do what I used to do with one." I believe he spoke for everyone who had common sense.

THE TESTAMENT

Rummaging one day through one of the closets at the far end of the hall on the fifth floor, looking for some standards document, I found an envelope left by someone who had left the company—as many did after so many years advancing against stone, while the wheels of commerce were accelerating on what everyone referred to as "the outside." The envelope contained "A Brief History of the Advanced Automation System." It was printed by hand and left behind, perhaps inadvertently, or perhaps with the hope that someone might some-day discover it and publish it. In every important way, it is the truth.

A young man, recently hired, devotes years to a specification written to the bit level for programs that will never be coded. Another, to a specification that will be replaced. Programmers marry one another, then divorce and marry someone in another subsystem. Program designs are written to severe formats, then forgotten. The formats endure. A man decides to become a woman and succeeds before system testing starts. As testing approaches, she begins a second career on local television, hosting a show on witchcraft. An architect chases a new technology, then another, then changes his mind and goes into management. A veteran programmer writes the same program a dozen times, then transfers. The price of money increases eight times. Programmers sleep in the halls. Committees convene for years to discuss key-stroking. An ambitious training manager builds an encyclopedia of manuals no one will use. Decisions are scheduled weeks in advance. Workers sit in hallways. Notions about computing begin in the epoch of A, edge toward B, then come down hard on A+B. Human factors experts achieve Olympian status. The Berlin Wall collapses. The map of Europe is redrawn. Everything is counted. Quality becomes mixed with quantity. Morale is reduced to a quotient, then counted. Dozens of men and women argue for thousands of hours: What is a requirement? A generation of workers retires. The very mission changes and only a few notice. Programming theories come and go. Managers cling to expectations, like a child to a blanket. Presentations are polished to create an impression, then curbed to cut costs. Then they are studied. The work spikes and spikes again. Offices are changed a dozen times. Management retires and returns. The contractor is sold. Software is blamed. Executives are promoted. The years rip by with no end in sight. A company president gets an idea: Make large small. Turn methods over to each programmer. Dress down. Count on the inscrutability of programming. Promote good news. Turn a leaf away from the sun. Maybe start over.

IBM RESPONSE TO FAA'S CURE LETTER: 12/10/92

IBM recommends . . . a new schedule, faster processors, and a new software development manager. The Chairman of the Board of IBM's Federal Systems Company [who was quoted later, "if people could have just left it alone, we could have delivered it"] will take over as IBM's AAS Program Manager. IBM will renew its efforts to test the software.

THE CURTAIN

When the project ended, the *Washington Post* reported that there were more than three thousand software defects in it. Other papers confirmed what everyone already suspected: the software could not be written. It was riddled with bugs.

Everyone was relieved. It was the software. It was the programmers, the way they programmed, and how they were managed, how loops were divined, and the assignment of numbers to variables, how modules were laid out, and how queues were allocated, and the time spent in the lab (was it enough?). The original software development manager had been the first to go. She was defamed, first from within and then outside, according to the rules of blame, written down nowhere, but embedded deep within our unconscious.

It was the software, of course. But not in the sense we all want to believe. It was in the nature of software, the nature of programming, its roots tangled in the mathematics of contradiction and logic and symbol production, plied by young tradesmen schooled in the tools of the latest process, its promise intensified by greed and ease, its complexity beyond imagining, man mingling with machine to a degree that cannot be described, felt to be immune to the laws of size — these computer programs, easy to miss within the great facilities that house them, amidst the spandrels and joists and treelike arches and great enclosures, decorated for art's sake.

As Harry once wrote: "Software is a source of both amusement and engineering achievement. It is easy to change, to the point of whimsy, and it allows us to do things heretofore unthinkable, like putting man on the moon. It is contradictory and miraculous. (Perhaps all miracles are contradictory.) As the genetic engineers and nanotechnologists well know, get far enough down into the world of symbols and one can transform the very nature of structure and meaning.

"Not satisfied with miracles, we want them to occur immediately: the Department of Defense has spent millions on productivity, and private companies sling their products out the door without hesitation, as if heaping more technological side effects on a planet already choked by them were not relevant. And, to boot, the trickier the nomenclature the better: we delight in giving old concepts new names, so that software remains, perforce, a field for the young. I believe the issue has been decided: once near-science has surrendered to cant."

I don't know how the programmers felt about the demise of the Advanced Automation System. I didn't ask them. Most of them had worked for years and knew as little about the forces at work as the Fijians knew about the causes of World War II. They worked too hard to know. Twenty-five-hour weekends. Sleepovers. In-plant baby-sitting. Afterward they left, ran to other jobs, any jobs. Many are on their second or third job now. They didn't leave for advancement; they left to get away. I don't know how they endured. They did good work. In the shank of the project, the suffocating bureaucracy and the beckoning of video games their friends in other places were creating in the new age of software did not affect them. They were a cadre of disciplined programmers, who would not cut corners on writing well-documented and thoroughly read and tested code, who wrote reliable programs, when they had every reason to give in to hurriedness. Or just give in.

CODA

"The Hearing before the Committee on Public Works and Transportation, Wednesday, April 13, 1994, 9:30 A.M." The Honorable David R. Hinson, Administrator, Federal Aviation Administration:

> This Subcommittee is well aware of the troubled history of the AAS program. The review . . . reflects a range of costs from $6.5 billion to $7.3 billion for completion of the program, and slippage of implementation dates by 9 to 31 months. I tasked the Center for Naval Analysis with conducting an independent 90-day review. I wanted that unvarnished look from an outside group.

The project ended quietly enough. A few articles appeared in the big-city newspapers, but civilization pretty much flowed on as usual. The Center for Naval Analysis performed its task and made its recommendations on cue, among them the "clear evidence that electronic flight strips were unnecessary; air traffic control companies that provide this capability found it necessary to provide paper strips." The all-digital approach would not do; too much automation, they reasoned. The FAA bit off more than it could chew. Put enough time and money into any project, up front, and it will fail.

In 1994, when the curtain fell, the FAA pressed Congress for help. Within months, Congress passed legislation permitting the FAA to waive the burdensome federal procurement regulations—over the protests of Senators John Glenn and Strom Thurmond, who argued that other government departments do just fine under the already streamlined rules. Senator William S. Cohen spoke out as well: "Regrettably, Congress bought the argument that federal procurement and personnel policies [personnel rules were reduced from 1,069 pages to 41 and 'integrated product teams' were put in place] have prevented the FAA from modernizing the air traffic control systems; but federal policies are not the problem. It was poor management."

Senator Cohen is mistaken. Poor management? For decades, the FAA has *managed* to keep the most complex system on Earth running 24 hours a day, 7 days a week. I know of no more competent and committed managers. Is management the problem down the block as well, at the IRS and FBI? The IRS management is being replaced because of software project overruns. The FBI is losing congressional support, not because of law enforcement problems but because of two software projects. I wonder where it will end. How many managers in how many departments in how many nations will be replaced because they were undone by the seduction of loops?

So, cumbersome regulations replaced software as the problem, its slate wiped clean. From now on, the FAA, unlike the Department of Defense—which must push on conservatively—can acquire systems without much oversight, so that, according to David Hinson, the past FAA administrator, the FAA can keep apace with industry. (If he meant the software industry, which is more and more taking on the character of alchemy, the problems of air traffic control may go from bad to worse.) Thus, the Advanced Automation System, failing to overhaul air traffic control automation, succeeded in restructuring the FAA. And, officially, we have learned nothing about the pitfalls of software and its use in large systems.

As for IBM, it sold the Federal Systems Company to Loral to raise cash. Loral would preside over a stripped-down version of the Advanced Automation System: the Display System Replacement, which turned defeat into victory. The Display System Replacement preserves much of the high-availability software and a version of the common console. But the mindless distributed approach is gone, as is the CHI. The controllers get new workstations, but the air traffic control data will look the same as it did in the original system, developed more than thirty years ago, including the paper flight strips. The system is now being deployed.

The principals, the IBM and FAA executives who conceived of the Advanced Automation System and ran the project, retired with handsome pensions, or, in some cases, moved on to equally high-paying jobs. As always, the consequences were felt at the bottom—with one exception. The only person at IBM who seemed to understand the project, whose financial acumen won the job for IBM and who ensured that IBM would make a profit through one replan after another, as well as upon termination, was John Cantwell, IBM's chief financial officer for the project. Shortly before the termination, John took a job with Computer Science Corporation, which had sought his talents for years.

After Loral took over, one of its executives, Bob Stevens, made a public announcement that the man most responsible for the failure of the Advanced Automation System was John Cantwell, and Loral had him removed. The statement was inaccurate as well as inappropriate. John was insightful, effective, and witty, and he was his own man: a rare combination. Unfortunately, less than two years later, shortly after he celebrated his fifty-first birthday, he died of liver cancer. Bob Stevens, who played a key role in the success of the Display System Replacement, got the air traffic control part of the company—now under Lockheed Martin—out of intensive care and back on its feet, running.

COMPUTING IS SELF-LIMITING

Journal Entry 113:

We may never recover from the beginnings of digital computing and programming as we understand it in the latter half of the twentieth century.

In spite of smaller and faster computer chips and designs that take advantage of parallel operations and the discovery of superconductivity, computing will remain at the mercy of its ancestral applications, as they have proliferated and will continue to proliferate through the next decades. The faster we create new computers and software and applications, the more must be absorbed, so that the old can be supported in the context of the new. We can barely keep up.

Soon, the simplest tasks will require computers one hundred times the speed and capacity of those built today. We cannot afford to pull the rug out from under the automation created just one or two or three decades ago. No institution, not the U.S. government, can afford to *replace* its automation; that is, to toss away the old model, like a used car, and buy a brand new one.

Computer programs are not Packards. Computer scientists who believe that computers will function like minds are onto something; not so much like minds as like species, forever evolving, spreading, adapting, coalescing, growing, until the individual program will seem to us like a single neuron in a single brain, something beyond our imagination, a name, an abstraction. What will occupy us will be the effects, the change in our behavior, in commerce, in communicating, in transportation, in medicine, in making war. But that is already self-evident, even to my cat, who of late has discovered that my wife's personal computer gives off heat and so prefers to lounge near the bits instead of in the bay window.

I know a man in Michigan. He developed a revolutionary approach to computing and programming. I promised him I would never reveal his name. I don't even know if he is still living. If he has died, his secrets have died with him. But that does not matter much. They are useless. We are stuck with the evolutionary pattern created by a hundred, then ten thousand, then millions of computing theoreticians and practitioners and users. There will be no starting over.

17

. . .

THE END-ALL OF PROGRAMMING

We will now discuss in a little more detail the struggle for existence.
—Charles Darwin, *The Origin of Species*

Marie's letter arrived late last spring, shortly after my neighbor ran his car through the end of his garage. I had never met Marie; I had never spoken to her. But she wrote to me from time to time, usually when Harry wasn't doing well. This time she stuck Harry's latest letter to me in her envelope.

She and Harry had been happy, she writes. But his expectations put a strain on their relationship. She says he thought too much. After they moved to Metz, Harry became preoccupied with a book he had bought, John McPhee's *Survival of the Bark Canoe*. Harry was always fascinated with trees and wood and he wanted to build a bark canoe like the ones built by Henri Vaillancourt, who McPhee describes in his book. Harry called his father and asked him to mail a copy of *The Bark Canoes and Skin Boats of North America*. Harry studied it like a monk.

One day Harry informed Marie that he had to go back to America to find wood. Birch and cedar and basswood. He was going to Maine, he said. The wood had to come from Maine. When he returned, Harry was buoyant. He had bought the wood, and it would arrive in a month. For that month, as Marie tells it, Harry hardly slept. He was working on the drawings for his canoe. He walked around Metz in the afternoons, visiting the cathedral. The canoe was beginning to clarify things for him.

Harry's last letter reads like that of a man on the edge of a recognition. It has the sound of a promise that's already been kept. He wanted to leave computers and programming behind, he said. "That's why I went to Africa."

For a good part of his life, Harry loved programming: "It has an organizing quality." He thought programming would help people, make life easier for them. That was in the beginning, when there were not too many programmers and he believed an easier life was a better one.

A few years back, Harry had written about the evenings in the 1960s when he sat in the computer room watching the lights on the computer's instruction address register, sometimes rippling fast like the keys of a player piano, sometimes frozen, as if they were staring back at him. He said the light show represented the relocated thoughts of our partying friends. The light show, he said, gave him the idea for a different approach to programming, an approach he worked on over the years, sometimes with insouciance, sometimes with the intensity of a warrior.

The problem is with the mathematics, he said. We program algorithms by compounding mathematical functions. One set of ordered pairs heaped on top of another and then another. "There is no N in and K out. There is no calculus of relations, as the mathematician Alfred Tarski puts it. No way to give a machine a simple request for information. Somehow humans and computers should be able to talk on our terms. Human knowledge in, human knowledge out, by way of the machine."

Harry made a big deal about the difference between data and information. He said we declared this the information age by watering down what we mean by information, which he believed was closer to the concept of news than gossip—something like "Hitler Invades Poland." Now *that's* news, according to Harry.

In the middle of the night, Marie writes, Harry went about augmenting the axioms of set theory: "With a broader definition of sets and set operations, the aspirations of humans and the fistlike operations of the computer can be reconciled with great efficiency. Today we meet the problem to be solved, and all of its variables—the fidelity of ground control of aircraft, the men and women who are paid to declare and define such problems, programmers, computers, power sources, physicists, couriers, the radius of the earth, and just about anyone or anything connected to the problem to the nth degree, past, present, and future—with raw computer data: a few values and a mountain of structural noise, the detritus of millions of operations. There is very little in the computer that is meaningful—unless you're a student of memory leaks, instruction streaming, or cache rates.

"The speed of computers has become an obstacle, as are most ends-in-themselves. With each passing year, we exchange addresses and pointers faster. The harder we dig for information, the more structure we inject. The more structure, the more we choke off and obscure the potential for meaning. We throw layer upon layer of code at the computer, then wade through it to get at values."

In one letter, Harry wrote about his longtime absorption in the theory of types. He believed that he could use his relational calculus to capture both the human's information needs and the computer's operations axiomatically and then map the two: "human to machine and machine to human." "The distance from the brain to the computer's circuitry covered in the straightest possible mathematical line. There will be no more paradigms and life cycles and structured this and structured that and schools of design. No more taking five years to do a season's work. It will work like a centrifuge, the values, the atoms of information, separating from the raw data. Then values combining as relations—the molecules. Then, finally, molecules combining as relationships, the proteins that give life to information."

Harry started with the computer. He didn't say which brand. He specified its operations in his new calculus, not just the arithmetic and the logic but channels and storage and clocks. A mathematically perfect representation, he believed. "Every operation and every bit is defined in terms of a set. When I'm finished, programs will be more reliable than the computers they run on."

He defined a problem, a banking problem, calculating accounts, and went about codifying it in sets, sets of accounts and money and credit and debt, all the elements of greed. Then he specified the mapping between the banking set and its operations and those of the computer. A giant morphism, he proclaimed it. When he was done, he had a system that learns as it runs. "When was the last time you asked the bank for your balance on June 3, 1987? They wouldn't know, because their system can't remember. Mine does. Every relation that is created is kept and available for further use. The system grafts 'relata'; a kind of technological pentimento. The longer it runs, the closer it gets to the universe of relationships. The system runs all the time, not just when you prod it. It organizes and verifies values and relations continually, looking for boundary conditions and inconsistencies. The past, the present, and the future oscillating under the math."

Marie writes that Harry got into trouble at his job. In Metz, he worked in a bank. His father is a banker and is quite wealthy. According to Marie, Harry would tap his father from time to time. Harry did well at the bank for a while. But he would get preoccupied with programming and skip work. Then his father would bail him out.

Marie also worried about Harry's eyesight. He had lost the vision in his right eye in a skiing accident. It was his brown eye. (Harry was born with one blue eye and one brown eye.) Marie claims that people with one blue eye and one brown eye have certain powers the rest of us lack. The Phoenicians, she says, were wary of women with eyes that didn't match. They kept their distance from them, lest they fall under their spell and be driven to slash their bodies. At any rate, it was the blue eye that concerned her. Harry would spend hours on his math and often complained about his vision. She feared he might go blind.

Harry tried to market his ideas. No one would listen to him about his axioms, about how he augmented set theory, how he used type theory to map the specifications of machine and program. He got his father to back him in a company, but he couldn't make a go of it. People want immediate results, Harry said. They hate theory. I told him once to lay off the theory. Show them the banking program. "It's not a program!" he insisted. "I'm not using that word anymore!" His approach was deemed impractical and inexplicable. Companies would ask him, What is a module? Harry would not answer. They would ask how one program calls another. Still he would be quiet. Harry, this is no way to win sponsors, I would tell him. Some companies were interested. They would bring in their experts, who would ask about error handling and data structures, and Harry would say that the structure is in the operations, and then leave.

Harry decided that if his ideas were to catch on, they would have to be embedded in a language so no one would notice them. "I have to invent a new programming language, one that maps relationships directly onto the computer—a new computer, which I will design, one that is mathematically pure. My set-theoretical machine operations will be part of the computer this time."

Of course, Harry could not design such a computer in any reasonable way. It would take far more than his own will and inspiration to build such a machine. But he tried anyway. He designed the language and the computer in concert, while he continued working on his canoe. He had almost no time for his wife and his friends and his work at the bank.

Harry made drawings of the computer design and the canoe. Sometimes, Marie writes, they would be folded together, as if they were part of a single architecture: the gunwales and integer sums; the stempiece and its relationship to partial correctness assertions, the head board and loops. Late in the afternoons, Harry would carve the birch. He worked on the center thwart first. He told Marie he didn't care how long it took him. He had no schedule. He kept the wood in an old barn near the western forts. My uncle had gone through there on the road from Verdun to Metz, before crossing into Germany at Prum, where he lost his leg near a winter sports resort north of Trier. There a relic of Christ's sandal is kept in the Baroque Salvatoribasilica.

As the mid-1990s approached, Harry detached himself further. He quit the bank altogether. The canoe was coming along. But the new computer-language project languished; Harry was becoming more depressed about automation.

His letter began: "Our world will become one large computer system. We will invent names upon names for the naming of names until meaning will become absorbed in the blue light of abstraction. Man shall ascend the edifice of types, pushing empathy forever downward into the dungeons of history. 'Extreme prejudice' that was once 'murder' and is now 'ethnic cleansing' will become a spool file. Third World countries will demand computer programs instead of food. Electronic cities will be built in the African desert and people will acclaim them. The Third and Fourth Worlds will give way to the Fifth." He quotes Genesis: "And the Lord said, Behold the people is one, and they have all one language; and this they begin to do: and now nothing will be restrained from them, which they have imagined to do."

Harry went on about "the silent syllables," the vocables of programming, how they will infiltrate the central nervous system of our kids—"more insidious than chemistry." A vast network of artificiality, mixing with the biological, until the distinction is lost, or not felt. Brain loops coiling through programming loops, running patterns around gene loops. Hooked on convenience, few will notice or care, he wrote. "Each generation bequeaths the side effects of its own technological comforts to its descendants. In the one great computer system, the side effects will prevail. An old woman will no longer hear Mozart, except for the occasional crackle of sound from her 50-year-old radio. Mostly, she will hear the din of her nephew, ribbing her about how often he urged her to replace her junk and buy up. 'What is your money for?' But she could not afford the great suites of hardware capable of playing the finest edition of *The Magic Flute*, now the only edition available, as newer and newer systems had replaced her broken phonograph and digital players of this or another age, now lying fallow, replacement parts ordered and forgotten by companies out of business, forsaken by the march of progress.

"Whither software: computer programs folding one into another, siring dark spots of unmerciful mass. It is inevitable. The great system will endure beyond the isotopes of plutonium, irreversible, like the Second Law."

Harry's letter went on for several pages, and I found myself turning back to Marie's words—how she felt she was losing her husband, or had lost him. Harry finished the canoe, Marie writes. He told her it was the first bark canoe ever built in Europe. It was about fourteen feet long and undecorated. One day in early September he told her he was going on a trip, taking the canoe to a lake. He had rented a room at the Chateau d'Alerville, southwest of Metz, about fifty-four kilometers east of Nancy, near Dieuze, along D199. He had written the owners, M. and Mme. L. Barthelemy. He would arrive on September 21. The lakes there are large enough to give the canoe a good trial. The morning he left Metz he reminded Marie about the carving knife—he had promised their neighbor he would loan it to him.

Mme. Barthelemy called Marie later in the week to tell her that Harry had gone out on the lake and not returned. He had been gone for over a day. She thought Harry was lost and called the police. Marie rented a car and phoned Harry's father.

The search went on for weeks. Then Marie and Harry's father packed his things in the chateau and drove back to Metz. Harry's father would sit there for hours and just shake his head, Marie writes. She told him she thought Harry did not drown, that he had gone away and would write her soon. Harry's father shook his head and went back to New York.

Marie says she never understood why Harry was so obsessed with computers. Programming: she has no idea what it is. She wants me to explain it to her someday. She misses Harry. She wonders what to do with his drawing and notes, his math and computer papers. Maybe she will ask someone in the museum. Or maybe I want them. She will stay in Metz in case Harry returns. Right now, she says, she doesn't want any more changes.

Marie didn't have to wait for long. Harry returned about a month later. He said very little about his trip. He sent me another letter. He writes that he had given a lot of thought to his ideas about computers and software and his life. He concluded that, despite his commitment to his ideas, spending the rest of his life on a different "technique" would either fail or he would go mad.

Instead, writes Harry, he loves Marie and the time he spends with her, and he loves working with the wood, because you can feel it and see it, and the things we make of it—cellos, canoes, statuary, are more natural than the things we make of computers. "Further, if I were to succeed somehow in building a better technique for introducing software into the world, I would be disappointed when it spurred man to expect and do more with it willy-nilly. Besides, my technique would do nothing to solve the analysis problem—deciding what to automate and why—or the management problem."

Harry and Marie are moving to New York. Harry will make his living in banking, with his father—part-time, so he can enjoy his life and continue woodworking. Harry writes that computers, programming, and software have had a grip on him too long. He will at last put that part of his life behind him.

AFTERWORD

. . .

The reader may be pessimistic on yet another score.
In this study no solution is put forward to the
problems raised.
— JACQUES ELLUL, *The Technological Society*

The term *creative nonfiction* has been coined for books such as this
one. Someone told me recently that it is the latest genre in literature.
If it is, I am happy to be part of it. I've always been a joiner. As I
understand it, writers have concluded that the twentieth century is
just too complex and incongruous to be described in terms of facts
alone. From what I have seen of it, I would agree.

As any serious logician would gladly grab you by the lapels and
explain to you, there is an important difference between not lying
and telling the truth. I am neither a logician nor a professional
writer, and I am neither a technical person nor a manager. I am a
passenger. I merely wanted to set down what I have seen and make it
entertaining. Like politics and baseball, the field of software is rich
in lore. Time and again, history—the events lived out—surpasses
our most savage imaginings. In this sequence of linked essays and

stories, I had no need to exaggerate. I was on hand and felt all of what I described. As we all learn, experiencing is far more painful or exhilarating than a secondhand telling. The truth is hard to get at because it cannot be separated from our feelings. The truth is hard to get at because we allow others to speak for us, through *their* feelings. That is the risk you and I are taking in sharing this book. I know you have your own book, and it is certainly different from mine.

Throughout this book I tried to remain silent with respect to my outright opinions, which is not to say that I remained neutral. I chose what I wrote and how I wrote it. I chose to describe one event over others. I have a point of view. Reading reviews of nonfiction books, in particular books about software and its development, I find that one theme dominates: people want answers. This may be why how-to books are far more popular than essays—which is a form rarely seen these days except in magazines. Although I prefer that people come to their own conclusions, I have been pressed by popular opinion to state my own. Thus, the Afterword.

It is my opinion that all of us try to learn about the nature of software and the nature of programming, and, for that matter, the nature of genetic engineering, molecular biology, and nanotechnology, any of the fields in which man can introduce the artificial into the natural world without much notice. Turning the world over to symbol producers will give us no time to recover from the inevitable side effects that, while making the world more convenient, erode its natural beauty. With the rise of personal computing and networks, more artificiality has been unleashed upon the planet in the past twenty years than in the previous forty thousand. You just can't see it.

I have read articles and heard speakers declare that two kinds of software are emerging: software that is not life-critical, such as games; and software that is life-critical, such as the programs that control nuclear power plants and banking systems. The two kinds of software have given rise to two development approaches: the first favoring creativity and managed in a laissez-faire style; the second, befitting its objectives, stressing more formality and engineering concepts.

I, like Harry, believe that this is a dangerous point of view. Unlike bridges, which are virtually impossible to combine because man cannot overcome the sheer magnitude of geographical space (imagine the Golden Gate Bridge somehow merging with the footbridge behind your beach house!), programs, resident across the globe, can be combined with relative ease. Topography and tectonics are no obstacle. Digital artifacts have boiled off what to us once appeared as huge gulfs of space and time.

Over time, there will be *one* system. According to Gresham's Law, the rarer and more precious software will become absorbed by its lesser and more prevalent kin. This is already happening. In the recently deployed FAA Display Replacement System, which replaces our en route air traffic controller's situation displays, the bridges supporting the IBM token ring local area network—that connects the displays to one another and to the central computers—consist of IBM PS/2s running DOS. Systems are most vulnerable at the joints, as are we. In this safety-critical system, the commercial operating system with the least pedigree and the least robustness regulates its hinges.

I recommend that a single approach be used to develop *all* software: an approach that applies as many of the classical methods of architecture and engineering as can be applied to software development, its use, and its maintenance. Further—as in the case of the major ground transport bridges in the United States—I hope that most of the software systems have been written, and need only be updated. The less software we invent, the better. Software for its own sake will compromise our planet's hygiene as surely as chemicals and missiles.

ANALYSIS AND RATIONALE

This brings me to the first of several recommendations regarding software development, all of which can be found in one form or another in classical engineering.

Before any software product or system is proposed, whether renovated or new, commercial or government, it must be justified.

Engineers should conduct a thorough analysis of the need (or, more accurately, the want) for the product or system. The analysis should include and document the political, economic, geographical, and social considerations, and all of the physical constraints, such as weather and power, as well as the logistical limitations. The analysis should clearly state the objectives of the product or system as an integral part of deriving its functions. The origins of what the product or system will do must be clear to builders, users, and historians. "Why?" is the most important question we can ask.

Through reasoning and experience, each objective should be qualified by one or more measures of effectiveness, so that, once designed, built, or purchased, the descendants of the objective, realized in one or more parts, can be evaluated. These measures, which also circumscribe the functions and constrain them, run the gamut from reliability to accuracy to responsiveness to the less obvious: Can the objective be realized at all? A proposal to build a bridge across the Straits of Gibraltar has undergone no less study for decades. Still, a decision has not been made. Imagine the consequences of joining Africa to Europe at its western promontory. Can we foretell them all?

The analysis and its recording cannot continue indefinitely. It should be bounded and yet inclusive, brief and yet rich in substance: enough to write clear and verifiable requirements. Narrative, flow diagrams, scenarios, equations, and the impact of the prospective automation on human procedures—the computer-human interface: all should be rendered concisely.

Over the years, systems engineering and software documentation, including operational concepts, requirements, and specifications of all kinds, has suffered from obesity. Much of the volume results from bloated outlines, running to five or six levels; irrelevant documentation standards—the so-called boilerplate; and a writing style that is seldom plain. Even books *about* software, its development and management, run to 300 and 400, sometimes 500, pages. When you think of documentation, do not consider the two-hour speech of Edward Everett at the commemoration of the Gettysburg National Cemetery on November 19, 1863. Think, instead, of the two-minute speech that followed it.

SPECIFYING

Having assured ourselves that the planet and our descendants will be better off, it is crucial that we write down our intent, that we specify as precisely as possible what the product or system will do *and what it will not do*. The latter is rarely recorded. Usually it is left to the imagination of programmers.

There can be no benchmark for correctness, or, stated in broader terms, for dependability and quality, without declaring intent. But we must be prepared to modify it. No one can foresee perfectly how a digital system will behave, or how we would like it to behave. Odd things occur. Our habits and procedures might change while the software is being built and it will no longer fit our conventions.

The fluctuation between intent and use has cursed architects for centuries. Buildings can be seen; and we have centuries of experience with them. With software, many of our original intentions will likely not see the light of day. Here, another technique used in classical engineering can be decisive: prototyping, especially with the often overwhelming and sensational graphics that now meet humans halfway in our use of automation. But prototyping should be engaged to learn, not to sell the prototype. Prototype software is just that. It is not a finished product. With the proper mix of formal expression and experimentation, based on a clear understanding of the objectives, the risk of wasting money — or worse, creating undesirable side effects — can be reduced.

Specifying should not end with the elaboration of a system's or product's functions and constraints. If software is bought over the counter, the documentation should be readable and informative. Although software vendors would not want to provide to users all levels of specification and design, it is prudent, even necessary, to provide such documentation to other suppliers or contractors who might have to integrate, test, and debug it in concert with other software. In this situation, supplying test cases and test data would also be helpful.

Commercial software should be guaranteed and warrantied, and certified in a manner similar to the drug trials conducted by the Federal Drug Administration and, in the case of physical artifacts, by the Underwriters Laboratory. (This applies to custom-built software as well.) The notion that software is a service that can be licensed at the user's risk is grave and irresponsible. When trains collide because the switching system uses a piece of commercial software, the terms and conditions of which declare that the user is responsible, who, beside the victims, will have blood on their hands?

To specify the system or product in the large is not enough. A software architecture and development plan should describe the rules for designing, developing, integrating and testing, maintaining, and managing the system. The architecture and development plan should be written concisely; they need not take 300 pages.

Specifications for each software subsystem should be written in the interest of maintaining intellectual control, if nothing else. The size of the project and the system or product in the making determine how many levels of specifying are needed. On large systems, subsystems may be composed of subsystems; on small systems, they may simply consist of modules. Nevertheless, specifications should be written as if lives depended on them. The interfaces between subsystems and modules should be defined as precisely as possible — all interfaces at every level, both functional and structural. Threads, or the typical scenarios that traverse subsystems and modules, should be identified and documented. Threads are especially informative in specifying software that is distributed over a number of computers. Threads are useful not only to designers and programmers but also to the staff that is responsible for modeling the product or systems and collecting performance measurements, as well as to those who will test the software.

Modules and procedures should be specified as well. Here the predicate or propositional calculus is useful, because it sets the stage for theorem proofs, if the stakes are high enough—and they always are. Surely, we should specify the pre-, post-, and invariant conditions of all loops. Short of that, I would settle for clearly commented code.

On the matter of keeping specifications up to date, I would prefer that they be modified from the top down, not after the fact.

MODULES, ORGANIZATIONS, AND INTEGRATION

Modularity is basic to engineering. In programming, the standards for modules vary. Often, a programming language or a method, such as Hoare's axiomatic approach, makes the definition of a module obvious. Modules create interfaces, both technical and human. Creating interfaces is not the purpose of modules; it is an inevitable side effect. Interfaces are the price we pay for breaking the work down, so that many people can work on small, manageable pieces of what may someday become the U.S. air traffic control system or an international banking system.

Whether you consider it the job of management or of architects, an art or a science, the mapping of modules and entire subsystems of modules to organizations is one of the decisive acts in engineering. If the alignment of thought and deed is not pure, confusion will mount exponentially. A good module is not a good module just because it is easy to compile, or even because its behavior is homogeneous, or because "small is beautiful"; it is a good module because it is obviously the work of one mind, one human being, whom everyone in the organization recognizes as its owner.

Integration is one of the most overused words in the field of digital systems. Integration is a complex undertaking that arises from the many levels of abstraction and refinement involved in our work, in concert with the division of thought and labor at each level. Integration is not an activity that begins after modules—be they hardware or software—have been built or bought. Integration begins with the analysis of wants, objectives, functions, and requirements. It continues through each level of refinement and never ceases, unless the product or system is retired. An entire volume could be written about this word and what it means. I will limit my thoughts to this. An integration plan should be written. It should describe how functions, subsystems, modules, databases, networks, commercial and customized hardware and software, the entire set of parts, will be combined, in what sequence, in what parcels, using what resources—including the organization, laboratories, and tools—and under what constraints and dependencies.

INSPECTIONS

Henry Petroski, in his article "New and Future Bridges" (*American Scientist*, November-December 1998), writes: "Engineering, like science, progresses through peer review."

I cannot improve on this statement. I will add only that, if inspections and peer reviews are crucial to classical science and engineering, should we expect no less in the field of computer programming and software development, in which the bulk of our work involves producing symbols? Like testing or any verification technique, inspections, be they applied to requirements, designs, code, test cases, or manuals, make the invisible visible; and they create milestones. Inspections not only save lives but are fundamental to getting the work done on time and knowing it.

TESTING AND EXPERIMENTAL SCIENCE

Testing is one of the major tenets of engineering. In my experience, however, it is the least emphasized aspect of software development. The roots of computer science as taught in universities (and most programmers are now drawn from graduates majoring in computer science) lie in applied mathematics—specifically, discrete mathematics. The subjects stress algorithms, digital design, queuing theory, recursion and compilers, networking (I am now reading from my copy of the Johns Hopkins syllabus), neural networks, expert systems, image processing, security, and data compression. No courses are devoted exclusively to testing.

One might infer that all of the courses include a healthy dish of experimentation, or what we simply call testing. I teach at the university; they don't.

As with inspections, I will not repeat what I have written about testing in the body of the book. I will add only this. Having studied the data from a number of large projects over 30 years, the projects that planned for and spent 60 percent or more of their technical budgets on verification—in the form of inspections, proofs, and the various levels of testing, from the software procedure to the system entire—have succeeded. Those that did not overran their schedules and budgets, or produced such shoddy goods that they were hardly, if ever, used.

Success these days is a relative term. Some products and systems get by simply because a very small portion of them are used. And then there are the help desks used by the commercial software houses. Staffing them must be cheaper than testing. As for the Apollo and Shuttle space projects, the management plan did not call for help desks.

Another element may explain why good things happen to bad software. I quote François Jacob's *The Possible and the Actual*: "What becomes actualized is progressively developed during life by interaction with the environment." Given enough failures and enough time and a sufficient number of patient users, why should a company invest heavily in testing?

MANAGEMENT

Management is engineering of the first order, whether financial, organizational, or technical. Management, no less than bridge building, is a matter of analysis and synthesis. It is a matter of expansion, then contraction and expression. The variables are abstract: money, the health and future of an organization and the people that compose it, time, the current social mores influencing labor and its contract with the production of goods, and techniques.

In Chapter 7, The Impossible Profession, I outlined some of the software management techniques that can keep programming on track: planning the particulars—or planning *as* particulars; and imposing the laws of classical production on the lawlessness of computer programming, including the earned value system and managing reserves.

The challenge is to integrate over the variables. We are underrunning the budget in Department A and behind schedule. Their modules have not been fully tested, yet they interface with the modules developed by Department B, whose budget has been overrun and which will soon be impacted by changes in requirements. The lead programmer in Department B has just found a job with another company, but several of her very capable subordinates will not work overtime. It is December 20. And so on. It's like that every week and, often, every day. A typical engineering problem.

The question arises, What data, and how much, do we need to collect to know where we stand? Just enough to affect the decisions of managers, no more and no less. Collecting so-called metrics for the sake of collecting them plays no part in successful production. Collecting data is part of the engineering framework, the feedback loop that circumscribes the potential and the actual, the management engine. Measurement is a matter of context.

WILL PROFESSIONAL PROGRAMMING BECOME A FORM OF ENGINEERING?

No. Some aspects of programming will remain forever beyond the grasp of classical engineering. Programming is too much like writing, too personal and private, too much under the spell of hyperbole, marketing, and self-aggrandizement. That is not to say that programming should not be more formal, more mathematical, where its roots lie. It is unlikely that software development and integration will attain the stature of classical engineering, including professional certification. This should not deter companies and individuals from using the engineering elements I have described above. We should not give up because there is no unified field theory of software engineering. The elements may not be easy to implement, but they are relatively simple, especially when compared with the study of proteins. As I see it, the problem is not that we do not know enough. The problem is that we do not practice what we know.

READING LIST

· · ·

I have included a list of books that I read and consulted during the writing of this book. It is not a bibliography. I refer to some of the books in the text; I recommend all of them. The articles and papers I consulted are too numerous to mention.

Alexander, Christopher, *Notes on the Synthesis of Form*

Alexander, Christopher, *The Timeless Way of Building*

Arbib, Michael A., *Brains, Machines and Mathematics*

Arbib, Michael A., and Manes, Ernest G., *Algebraic Approaches to Program Semantics*

Barrow, John D., *Pi in the Sky*

Bateson, Gregory, and Mary Catherine, *Angels Fear*

Bateson, Gregory, and Mary Catherine, *A Sacred Unity*

Birkerts, Sven, *The Gutenberg Elegies*

Bolter, J. David, *Turings's Man*

Brock, William H., *The Norton History of Chemistry*

Brooks, Frederick P., *The Mythical Man-month*

Campbell, Jeremy, *Grammatical Man*

Crossley, J. N., *What Is Mathematical Logic?*

Davis, Philip J., and Hersh, Reuben, *The Mathematical Experience*

Ellul, Jacques, *The Technological Society*

Gould, Stephen Jay, *Ever Since Darwin*

Gries, David, *The Science of Programming*

Haack, Susan, *Philosophy of Logics*

Henry, Granville C., *The Mechanism and Freedom of Logic*

Ince, D. C., *An Introduction to Discrete Mathematics and Formal System Specification*

Jacob, François, *The Possible and the Actual*

Leibniz, G. W., *New Essays on Human Understanding*

McCulloch, Warren S., *Embodiments of Mind*

Minsky, Marvin L., *Computation: Finite and Infinite Machines*

Monod, Jacques, *Chance and Necessity*

Noble, David F., *The Religion of Technology*

Petroski, Henry, *To Engineer Is Human*

Quine, Willard Van Orman, *The Ways of Paradox and Other Essays*

Quine, Willard Van Orman, *Word and Object*

Sale, Kirkpatrick, *Rebels Against the Future*

Sawyer, W. W., *Mathematician's Delight*

Schumacher, E. F., *A Guide for the Perplexed*

Schumacher, E. F., *Small Is Beautiful*

Sheldrake, Rupert, *The Presence of the Past*

Shepheard, Paul, *What Is Architecture?*

Simon, Herbert A., *Models of Bounded Rationality*

Sommerhalder, R., and van Westrhenen, S. C., *The Theory of Computability*

Thomas, Lewis, *The Lives of a Cell*

Thomas, Lewis, *The Youngest Science*

Thompson, Simon, *Type Theory and Functional Programming*

Weizenbaum, Joseph, *Computer Power and Human Reason*

Whitehead, Alfred North, and Russell, Bertrand, *Principia Mathematica to * 56*

Wieger, L., *Chinese Characters*

Wittgenstein, Ludwig, *Tractatus Logico-Philosophicus*

ADDITIONAL COPYRIGHT INFORMATION

• • •